Tips & Traps
for Remodeling Your Attic,
Basement, and Garage

About the Author

R. Dodge Woodson has been involved in the building trades for 30 years and has been a self-employed contractor for 25 years. He is the owner of The Masters Group, Inc., a general contracting, remodeling, and plumbing firm in Maine. Woodson has written dozens of books on the industry for both consumers and professionals.

Tips & Traps
for Remodeling Your Attic,
Basement, and Garage

R. Dodge Woodson

6 4 3 . 7
W 898 †

McGRAW-HILL

New York   Chicago   San Francisco   Lisbon   London   Madrid
Mexico City   Milan   New Delhi   San Juan   Seoul
Singapore   Sydney   Toronto

The **McGraw·Hill** *Companies*

1 2 3 4 5 6 7 8 9 0   DOC/DOC   0 1 0 9 8 7 6

ISBN-13: 978-0-07-147557-0
ISBN-10: 0-07-147557-5

The sponsoring editor for this book was Cary Sullivan and the production supervisor was Pamela A. Pelton. It was set in Garamond by Lone Wolf Enterprises, Ltd. The art director for the cover was Handel Low.

Printed and bound by RR Donnelley.

Interior photo images courtesy of photos.com.

McGraw-Hill books are available at special quantity discounts to use as premiums and sales promotions, or for use in corporate training programs. For more information, please write to the Director of Special Sales, McGraw-Hill Professional, Two Penn Plaza, New York, NY 10121-2298. Or contact your local bookstore.

 This book is printed on recycled, acid-free paper containing a minimum of 50% recycled, de-inked fiber.

This book is dedicated to Adam and Afton, the two brightest stars in my life.

Contents

Foreword

Are you thinking of hiring a general contractor for home improvements or remodeling? Has the thought of saving thousands of dollars by being your own general contractor crossed your mind? Most homeowners seeking to improve their homes either hire a general contractor or act as their own construction manager while hiring subcontractors. In either case, this book is one of the most important tools that will be found on the job site.

Adding space to your home or improving existing living conditions can be a very traumatic time. But, it doesn't have to be. With the right knowledge, you can maintain control of your job. It will be easier on you to hire a general contractor, but there is a lot of money to be saved if you act as your own general contractor.

Almost anyone researching the rules of the road for remodeling has discovered horror stories about doing business with contractors and subcontractors. These stories are true. R. Dodge Woodson, the author, has been in the business for 30 years. He shares many of his own experiences between these pages. Best of all, he tells readers what to watch out for and how to avoid costly mistakes before, during, and after a home improvement or remodeling job.

Woodson has compiled a career of information here to help and protect you. For the mere cost of this book, you may save thousands of dollars on your job. Even more important, it is likely that you will avert disaster by not making the types of mistakes that many homeowners and inexperienced general contractors make.

Thumb through these pages. Notice the bullet lists, the tip boxes, and the numerous sample forms. The author has taken a serious, complicated subject and turned it into an accessible, easy-to-understand guide for homeowners. The writing is concise and the illustrations point out key factors toward a successful job.

You don't have to be a victim of unscrupulous contractors. Woodson will show you how to avoid them. Additionally, you will learn how to manage reputable contractors and assure yourself of quality work that comes in on budget and on time. Your home may be your single largest investment; don't risk it to renegade contractors. Learn how to protect yourself, your finances, and your home with this reader-friendly roadmap to success.

Go ahead and spend a little time looking over the chapters. It will not take long to see the value of Woodson's invaluable experience and advice. You don't have to go it alone. Take the words of a veteran contractor with you along every step of your remodeling adventure. Pick and choose the topics that you need, but don't go home without this essential element of your new project.

Tips & Traps
for Remodeling Your Attic,
Basement, and Garage

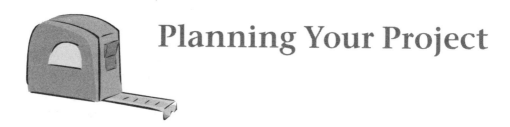

1

Planning Your Project

Proper planning is an essential element to a successful remodeling project. Without good planning your budget can be busted and your job can lack appeal. This chapter is going to teach you how to develop plans, material take-offs, and estimates. While these facets of your job do not require a hammer or nails, they are equally as important as the more hands-on parts of the job.

GENERAL PLANNING

General planning is the normal starting point of any remodeling task. This planning can involve everything from what color paint you will use to how much money you can afford to spend. Let me give you a few examples of the types of questions you may wish to ask yourself.

For this example, assume you are considering converting the upstairs of your garage into a bedroom. Your garage is 24' x 24' and it is attached to your home. Now for the questions that may arise.

> **TRADE TIP**
>
> When you are planning your remodeling project, you must keep in mind the minimum requirements for ceiling height. These measurements can vary from one building code to another, so check with your local code office before you invest much time or money into your project. If you don't have enough ceiling height, your project may not be able to go forward. However, it may be possible to apply for, and receive, a variance to allow you to move ahead. The key is to talk to your local code officer in advance.

How much ceiling height will you need? An eight-foot ceiling height is standard, but you could get by with a ceiling height of seven feet, six inches. A lower ceiling height probably would not pass local building codes, and it would have a detrimental affect on your property's appraised value.

Will you have to alter the pitch of your existing garage roof to obtain a satisfactory ceiling height? There is a good probability that you will. You can make this determination by measuring from the bottom of the ceiling joists in your garage to the finished floor level of your home. Remember to allow for the thickness of the new ceiling and flooring in your converted space.

If you are forced to alter the pitch on your garage roof, will the added pitch interfere with existing windows in your home? As you increase the roof pitch, the roof will reach higher onto the side of your home. Will altering the roof pitch leave unsightly areas in your home's siding, where the old roof attached to the house?

How will you get new electrical wiring into the converted space?

> **PRO POINTER**
>
> Adding new electrical circuits, new heat zones, or new plumbing can require extensive and expensive upgrades to existing systems. Be sure to confirm the capabilities of your existing systems with the proper experts prior to making any commitments.

Will you be installing a bathroom in part of the space? If so, how will you get the plumbing into the area above the garage? Will your home's existing building drain and sewer handle the increased load of a new bathroom? In most areas, a three-inch building drain is not allowed to carry the waste from more than two toilets.

Adding a third toilet could mean replacing your sewer or parts of your building drain.

As you can see, we have barely scratched the surface, but important questions are arising quickly. The planning stage of your project is no small task. If you do your planning properly, it will save you time and money. If you do it wrong, you will regret it for years to come.

Your general planning requirements will vary, depending on the nature of your project. However, if you start at the bottom and work your way up, you have a good chance of catching any big problems before they happen. One good way of doing this is by working with a checklist.

Your checklist should have a spot for every phase of work you anticipate doing. As you go through your planning, you can check off the areas you have already covered. It doesn't hurt to have professionals come in to give you bids and render advice. Even if you do the work yourself, the pros may point out issues you neglected.

Keep resale value in mind when planning your conversion. A feature you love may not be appreciated by future home buyers and appraisers. You should strive to avoid functional obsolescence. For example, if your only access to your new attic living

PRO POINTER

Your general planning requirements will vary, depending on the nature of your project. However, if you start at the bottom and work your way up, you have a good chance of catching any big problems before they happen. One good way of doing this is by working with a checklist.

TRADE TIP

Keep resale value in mind when planning your conversion. A feature you love may not be appreciated by future home buyers and appraisers.

DID YOU KNOW?

One of the first steps in a remodeling plan is establishing a viable budget. You must know how much you can afford to spend before you begin planning your work. How would it feel to come up with the plan of your dreams only to find out that it is far more expensive to complete than you can afford? Establish a working budget before you invest too much time in your improvement project.

space is a spiral stairway, how will you get furniture into the space? While spiral stairs add a touch of flair and are a reasonable second means of access, they are not the preferred choice as the only means of access.

Most people are restricted in their desires by the reality of their budgets. It is fine to dream of grandiose plans, but when the time comes to pay for your plans, the dream may turn into a nightmare. The best way to avoid overspending is by obtaining solid estimates on all your expenses, including the hidden expenses. To do this, you need plans and material take-offs.

DRAWING FLOOR PLANS

Drawing floor plans does not always require an architect. In small jobs, you may be able to draw your own plans. In some cases, a draftsperson or even your local lumber supplier may be able to produce the plans. The most important factor is to have a set of working plans.

If you are only finishing off a basement, and not affecting the structural integrity of your home, you should be able to draw your own plans. Converting your garage may also be possible with home-drawn plans. But, when it comes to adding dormers and performing major structural work, consult a professional.

For small jobs, a simple line drawing may be all you need for plans. As the degree of difficulty escalates, so does the need for more detailed plans and specifications. Many lumber suppliers will provide you with detailed working plans when you buy your supplies from them. The cost for these plans is minimal. On the other hand, if you have an architect

---

PRO POINTER

What should be included in working plans? As much information as you can get in them. The more detailed the plans are, the less likely you are to have a problem down the road. Cross-sections and details are usually a part of working plans for major jobs. These detail sections can show such items as stairs or wall cut-throughs. A joist detail will show the placement, spacing, and size of floor joists. A truss detail will identify the type of truss to be used and pertinent information about the truss.

draw your blueprints, be pre-
pared to spend a sizable sum of
money.

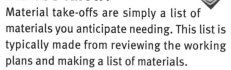

DID YOU KNOW?
Material take-offs are simply a list of materials you anticipate needing. This list is typically made from reviewing the working plans and making a list of materials.

What should be included in
your working plans? As much
information as you can get in
them. The more detailed the
plans are, the less likely you are
to have a problem down the road. Cross-sections and details are usually a part of working plans for major jobs. These detail sections can
show such items as stairs or wall cut-throughs. A joist detail will show
the placement, spacing, and size of floor joists. A truss detail will
identify the type of truss to be used and pertinent information about
the truss.

MATERIAL TAKE-OFFS

Material take-offs are simply a list of materials you anticipate
needing. This list is typically made from reviewing the working plans
and making a list of materials. Professionals are usually quite capable
of preparing accurate take-offs, but the responsibility can leave the
inexperienced wondering what went wrong.

Most people who are not accustomed to making take-offs will
leave out many needed components. For example, the average person
would probably not figure the amount of dead wood needed to
frame a dormer. Nails are often overlooked, as are adhesives and similar less apparent needs. The omission of these small items can add
up to substantial money.

One way to develop a material list is to ask your lumber supplier
to do it for you. Most suppliers are willing to provide material lists
from your plans, but the quality of their lists may leave something to
be desired. There are two factors working against you under these circumstances. Some suppliers will casually forget a few items in order
to make their price quote more attractive. Even well-meaning suppliers are likely to be in a rush and miss items you will need. The old
saying, "you get what you pay for" may be appropriate in this case.

Since the supplier is not usually being paid to develop a material list, it stands to reason that the quality of the list may not be great.

If you are having your plans drawn by an architect or drafting firm, you may be able to arrange for these people to create an accurate take-off. Since these people are getting paid, and they don't have a stake in your material purchases, they are more likely to render an unbiased and more accurate list.

The best way to arrive at an accurate material take-off is, if you have the ability, to do it yourself. Depending upon the quality of your plans, this may not be such a demanding task. Many blueprints go into great detail. They show joist diagrams and headers. They show electrical boxes and wiring routes. If you have such detailed plans, making a good take-off is not difficult.

If you elect to figure your own material list, you will benefit from some of these pointers:

- Pick a set of plans to be used for the primary purpose of doing a take-off.

- Use a check-list to reduce the likelihood of missed items.

- As you count items, circle them with a red pencil. This will help you to avoid duplication of items and will make it easy to see if you have forgotten anything.

- When you think you have calculated all of your materials, add a percentage of materials for waste and mistakes. By adding a percentage, say five percent, to your lumber list, you are less likely to run short of material or money.

- An ideal way to come up with the most accurate take-off is the use of combined methods. First, do your own take-off. Then, have your building supplier perform a take-off. If feasible, have the person that drew the plans, if it wasn't you or your material supplier, generate a material list. Then, compare all of the lists and look for discrepancies. I'm certain you will find some.

- After comparing all of your lists and noting all differences, investigate to see which lists are right and which ones are incorrect.

By using this comparative method, you assure the most accuracy you can hope for.

ESTIMATES

The next step is obtaining estimates for all labor and material to be used in your job. If you are doing all of the work yourself, the labor aspect may not be important to you, but you still might want to look at the time you will be spending on different phases of the work. Let me give you an example.

As a professional builder and remodeler, I have never found a way to install insulation that was more cost effective than subbing it out to an insulation contractor. For whatever the reason; and I assume it is the price these contractors pay for their materials, I have never been able to justify doing my own insulation work. This doesn't disappoint me because I despise working with insulation, but it is an interesting fact.

By looking at how much time you will spend on certain phases of your job, you may discover that your time is more valuable following some other pursuit. This, of course, is a personal decision, but it is worth considering.

DID YOU KNOW?
Hiring professionals to do your work in the trades is often more cost effective than doing the work yourself, if you have adequate income opportunities in your profession.

MATERIAL PRICES

Let's start with material prices. Once you have an accurate take-off, getting quotes on your material prices is easy. All you have to do is circulate your material list among suppliers and request a formal quote. Note that I said a formal quote, not an estimate. Most material suppliers will quote prices that are good for at least thirty days. Get your quotes in writing and compare them closely. Simply looking at the bottom line can be a big mistake.

The bottom-line figure can be deceiving. If the supplier has omitted items or substituted items, the price quoted will not be a fair comparison with other bidders. Check each quote, item-by-item, to be sure they are competitive bids.

LABOR PRICES

Labor prices, if you need to obtain them, are more difficult to compare. It is easy to get three bids from different plumbers, but not all plumbers are the same. Here are some key issues to consider in the sub-contractors you decide to use:

- Insurance is a major issue. A contractor without adequate insurance is a strong liability to you. What happens if an electrician burns your house down or a plumber floods your home? If these contractors are not insured, where will the money for repairs come from?

- All contractors should have basic liability insurance. If the contractor has employees, workers compensation insurance is normally required.

- You can confirm a contractor's insurance coverage by asking the contractor for a certificate of insurance. These certificates should come to you through the mail, from the insurance company, not the contractor.

- Once you are satisfied that the contractors bidding your work are reputable, stable, and properly insured, you have much of the battle won. However, it is still not easy to compare bids for labor.

- Beware of contractors who give you hourly rates for doing the job.

- It is almost always best to get a firm contract price.

- When you allow a contractor to work at an hourly rate, the costs can get out of hand.

- By working with written contracts, you can control the costs of your job.

- One of the hardest parts of comparing contractors is the quality of their work.

- Try to arrange to see finished examples of each contractor's work.

- The process of choosing the best contractors can be time consuming and frustrating, but cutting corners on your research can have disastrous results.

HIDDEN COSTS

Hidden costs can sneak up on you. Beware of them. Here are a few types of problems that can creep up on you:

- Have you plugged in a number for the cost of your building, plumbing, electrical, and heating permits?

- Have you factored in a price for trash removal?

- If you are financing your job, have you calculated the fees involved with the loan, such as appraisals, title searches, and the like?

- Depending on the nature of your job, these hidden expenses can mount, costing you more out-of-pocket money.

PUTTING IT ALL TOGETHER

Once you have your plans, take-offs, and estimates, all that is left is putting it all together. By taking a second look at your plans, you may find subtle changes you want to make. Now is the time to make them. Making changes during the job can be very costly.

If you have compared your take-offs thoroughly, you should feel confident in your material needs. Your estimates, or better yet, quotes, will give you some comfort in the cost of your endeavor. However, don't be lulled into a false sense of security with your pricing information.

Labor and material prices do fluctuate. If your job is postponed or delayed, prices may change. It is also conceivable that certain materials or contractors will not be available when you need them. If this happens, you may have to go to your second choice. Going to the second choice often means spending more money.

If you have planned well, there will not be many unexpected costs. Even so, you should allow yourself a margin of error. Some contractors use a five-percent float factor and others use a slush pile of ten percent. You will be wise to allow at least this much, and probably more, to be sure you don't bust your budget.

OUTLINE OF WORK TO BE DONE

GARAGE CONSTRUCTION

Choose style of garage desired.
Draw a rough draft of garage or obtain a pre-drawn plan.
Make or obtain a list of required materials.
Select materials to be used.
Price materials.
Make list of contractors needed or a list of general contractors.
Contact contractors.
Obtain labor quotes.
Evaluate budget needs and ability to afford the garage.
Make financing arrangements.
Make final decision on plan to be built.
Choose contractors and check references.
Meet with attorney to draw-up contracts and other documents.
Make commitments to suppliers and contractors.
Schedule work.
Start work.
Inspect work.
Obtain copies of code enforcement inspections.
Make required payments and have lien waivers signed.
Inspect completed job.
Make punch-list, if necessary.
Make absolute final inspection and approval.
Make final payments, except for retainages.
Make retainage payments.

CATEGORIES OF WORK TO BE DONE

Survey	Framing	Painting
Blueprints	Windows	Electrical work
Permits	Doors	Insulation
Site work	Sheathing	Drywall
Footing	Roofing	Electric door openers
Foundation	Siding	Landscaping
Floor preparation	Trim work	
Floor		

FIGURE 1-1
A sample planning list for a garage construction.

COST PROJECTIONS

Item/Phase	Labor	Material	Total

Total estimated expense

FIGURE 1-2
Figuring cost projections.

2

Raising the Roof

If you are planning to convert the attic of your home or garage into living space, you may have to raise the roof. This is an expensive and complicated procedure, but sometimes it is the only way to make an attic into usable living space. Unless you are very handy and have some help available, this job is best left to professionals.

Why would you have to raise the roof? There are times when there simply isn't enough ceiling height to convert attic space into habitable space. Normally, a minimum ceiling height of seven-feet-six-inches is required by the building code. As with any rule, there are exceptions. For example, it is often permissible to have a finished ceiling height of only seven feet in a bathroom. Since many jurisdictions use different building codes and may interpret the codes differently, you should always check with the local code enforcement office before doing any major work.

ROOF TRUSSES

Another reason why you may be forced to build a new roof structure is the presence of roof trusses in your existing roof. Roof trusses are engineered to meet the requirements of their present use, not necessarily the additional requirements of adding living space. Since trusses are engineered and built to exacting standards, cutting or altering the trusses can weaken or destroy their structural integrity.

Attic trusses and room trusses are two types of trusses that you can work around to convert an attic to living space. These trusses are made with an open area in the center of the truss. This opening allows the freedom of movement between the trusses. Since most trusses have pieces of wood weaving through them, that prevents building a room; attic and room trusses overcome this obstacle.

Even with attic trusses, some additional support will be required to convert the attic to living space. This will normally require adding floor joists between the bottom plates of the trusses. Room trusses, on the other hand, are intended to be converted into living space. However, check the structural rating to be sure it is adequate for your proposed use.

ROOF PITCH

The existing roof pitch may not allow a feasible conversion of attic space. Roofs that have a low pitch offer a wide attic floor area, but a short ceiling height. A steep roof pitch provides good head room, but makes for a narrow room.

ROOF DESIGNS

Roof designs can play large roles in the ease of attic conversions. One of the best types of design to

DID YOU KNOW?
If you have any type of truss, other than attic or room trusses, they will have to be removed completely. This, of course, will mean substantial damage to the ceilings in the rooms below.

FIGURE 2-1
A work in progress. *(Courtesy of National Gypsum.)*

work with is a gambrel roof. The majority of houses have gable roofs. Gable roofs are okay for attic expansion, but they often require the addition of dormers, if a lot of finished space is desired. A hip roof provides a good center height, but it suffers in ceiling height around the exterior walls. Of all the most common roof designs, the gambrel allows the most potential for expansion, without the use of dormers.

Since gambrel roofs make the most sense, this is the type of roof we will explore throughout this chapter. If you are going to replace your entire roof structure, you might as well get the most for your money. Now, let's look at the specifics of raising the roof.

TRUSSES VERSUS RAFTERS

When you are considering raising your roof, the first question to address is the one of trusses versus rafters. Take a look in your attic and see which type of roof system you presently have. If you have a

Rafter size (inches)	Spacing (inches)	Pine (feet/inches)
2 × 4	12	11-6
2 × 4	16	10-6
2 × 4	24	8-10
2 × 6	12	16-10
2 × 6	16	15-8
2 × 6	24	13-4
2 × 8	12	21-2
2 × 8	16	18-10
2 × 8	24	17-104
2 × 10	12	24-0
2 × 10	16	23-8
2 × 10	24	21-4

FIGURE 2-2
Typical maximum spans for roof rafters.

stick-built roof system, one with rafters, you should be able to salvage the existing joists. You may also be able to use much of the lumber from the old rafters. If you have any type of truss, other than attic or room trusses, they will have to be removed completely. This, of course, will mean substantial damage to the ceilings in the rooms below.

The ceilings in the rooms below will be attached to the joists in the attic floor. When you remove trusses, you are removing an entire unit of roof support and ceiling joists. However, a stick-built system will have independent rafters and ceiling joists. They will be nailed together, but they may be separated. In either case, you are likely to experience significant damage to the ceilings below.

> **TRADE TIP**
> Homeowners who are contracting portions of their jobs out to professionals should give serious thought to letting professionals handle roofing work.

REMOVING THE OLD ROOF

If you decide to install a new roof, removing the old roof will be one of your first priorities. This, obviously, is a big job. Before you begin ripping off the old roof, there are a few factors to consider.

RAIN

What will you do if it rains before you get the new roof on? Well, this is a problem, even for professionals. One way to limit the effects of rain is with tarpaulins. Many professionals will work the roof in sections. They will remove and rebuild sections of the roof, rather than stripping off the whole roof and trying to replace it before rain comes. At night, the pros often cover the unprotected roof sections with waterproof tarps.

SAFETY BRACING

Safety bracing should be installed before the old roof covering is removed. A simple way to accomplish this is by nailing two-by-fours, horizontally, across the rafters or trusses. Ideally, you should run this bracing across the rafters or trusses at the bottom, center, and near the top. This ties the roof members together to provide strength when the roof sheathing is removed. The bracing should extend from one end of the roof to the other and on both sides of the attic. Without this bracing, the roof members may have little to no support once the roof sheathing is removed.

DID YOU KNOW?

Even if you are contracting all of your home improvement work to professionals, it pays to have a good idea of what to expect from the contractors. This will not only prepare you for what to expect, it will give you an edge in knowing that the contractors are doing what they should be doing and are not taking advantage of you.

REMOVING SHINGLES

Will you be removing the shingles? Yes, you will, but how you do it will depend on your approach to the job. Many people remove the shingles as one phase of the job. Other people remove the shingles and the roof sheathing all at one time. If you decide to remove the shingles individually, you will spend more time on your job.

When removing just the shingles, a common method to use is scraping. By using a long-handled scraper, you can place the blade of the scraper under the shingles and push them off the roof. You could use a putty knife to lift the edges of the shingles and pull them off, but the heavy-duty scraper will be much faster. These instructions are based on working with asphalt or fiberglass shingles.

If you happen to have a slate or tile roof, the procedure is more difficult. A tin roof is also removed differently. If you have a roof with one of these types of coverings, consult a local professional for recommended removal procedures. With all phases of your job, keep safety in mind. Wear safety glasses and appropriate clothing and footwear. It is best not to work alone, and always be aware of what is below you as the discarded roofing is falling to the ground.

REMOVING SHINGLES AND SHEATHING ALL AT ONCE

When you remove shingles and sheathing all at once, you save time and you are able to work from inside your attic, instead of outside, on the roof. A reciprocating saw is the best tool for this job, but a circular saw will work, it just is not quite as safe for most users.

Before conducting this procedure, it is important to block off the area around your home so no one will be injured by falling debris. Since you are inside the attic, you will not be able to see who or what is below. Also, be sure to have your bracing in place on the rafters or trusses.

Once the work area is secure, you are ready to remove the roof sheathing and shingles. With a rough, wood-cutting blade in your saw, cut the sheathing from inside the attic, along the edges of the rafters or trusses. Most rafters and trusses are set on two-foot centers. This means you will be cutting out sections of sheathing that are approximately two-feet wide.

It is usually best to cut these two-foot wide pieces out in sections, rather than in their full-length dimension. For example, if your rafters are 18 feet long, make the length of your cuts about four feet. These smaller pieces are more manageable and create less danger. Remember, even these small pieces are going to be heavy, and they are going to fall somewhere when cut loose. If you have a helper, this isn't much of a problem, but if you are working alone, extra caution is required. Once the sheathing and shingles are gone, you are ready to address the rafters or trusses.

REMOVING TRUSSES

Truss removal can be done in several ways. If you are willing to remove the ceiling in the rooms below your attic, the trusses can be lifted off the top of your house in one piece. However, this is usually not practical in most remodeling jobs. It is unlikely you will make it through the truss-removal process without damaging the ceilings below, but there is a way to minimize that damage.

The bottom cord of your trusses will be sitting on the top plate of your house. Add extra nails, normally 16d nails, to make the connection between the bottom cord and the top plate stronger. Once this is done, and your safety bracing is in place, you can cut out sections of the trusses. As you cut out the trusses, leave the bottom cord in place.

The bottom cord will help to maintain the integrity of the ceilings below. The new floor joists that you will be adding will be taller than the bottom cords. Also, the new joists will normally be set on sixteen-inch centers. The bottom cords should be on twenty-four-inch centers. This allows you to leave the bottom cords, without inhibiting the new joists.

RAFTER REMOVAL

Rafter removal is similar to truss removal, but it is generally a little easier. Rafters and ceiling joists are connected, but they are not an integral unit, like trusses. Rafters are normally nailed to a common ridge board. The ridge board is the board that runs the length of your attic, at the peak, and allows all of the rafters to lean into it and be nailed.

Rafters are generally notched to sit on the top plate of the house. The rafters are usually nailed to the top plate and to the ceiling joists. Before removing your rafters, place safety braces under the ridge board. These braces should run from the ceiling joists to the bottom of the ridge board. These braces are intended to support the ridge board as the rafters are removed.

Before beginning the demolition work, add some extra nails to the ceiling joists to hold them to the top plate. It is not a bad idea to cut blocking for installation between the ceiling joists. The blocking will minimize twisting and nail-pops in the ceilings below.

Start your rafter removal at the point where the rafter connects to the ceiling joist. Using a nail-puller, remove the nails holding the rafter to the ceiling joist. Next, remove the nails holding the rafter to the top plate. Then, remove the nails holding the rafter to the horizontal safety bracing. With these nails removed, all that is left are the nails at the ridge board. Once the ridge-board nails are out, you can lower the rafter to the ground.

PUTTING THE NEW ROOF ON

Once you have the old roof system removed, you are ready to install the new roof. You have two basic options. You can stick-build a new roof, or you can install room trusses. Let's look at how each procedure will work.

PRO POINTER

If you will need to position a crane or other equipment on the property of neighbors, secure their permission well in advance of beginning your project.

ROOM TRUSSES

If room trusses will serve your needs, they are the fastest way to get your new roof structure on. This procedure works best if you hire a crane and operator to set the trusses in place for you. If you don't have the benefit of a crane, plan on having some strong bodies to help pull the trusses to the top of the house. The trusses on each end of the house will be called gable trusses. They will be made differently than the rest of the trusses. These gable trusses will be built to allow siding to be installed on them.

Once the trusses are on top of the house, they are stood up and slid into position. This job requires extra hands. The trusses should be nailed to the top plate as they are put into place, and they should be braced with two-by-fours. As the line of trusses gets longer, the trusses should be tied together with horizontal bracing, just as described earlier. Once the trusses are up, they must be squared and nailed into their permanent position. Bracing should be left in place until the roof sheathing is installed.

STICK-BUILDING THE ROOF

Stick-building the roof is a little more complicated, but it is actually easier, in some ways, for a small work crew. Setting the ridge board is the most strenuous aspect of this type of roof framing.

The first step is to set the ridge board into place. The ridge board will have to be held into place with bracing and supports. Once the ridge board is in place, you are ready to install your rafters.

Most professionals figure their desired rafter design and cut them on the ground. The rafter will be notched to sit on the top plate. In the trade, this notch is often called a bird's-mouth. The piece of the rafter extending over the side of the house is called the tail, and it forms the overhang. The other end of the rafter will be angled to fit against the ridge board. Once you have cut one rafter that fits properly, you can use it as a template for your other rafters.

Once the rafters are cut, sit them in place, one at a time. Nail each rafter as you go. The rafter should be nailed to the ridge board, the top plate, and to the ceiling joists. You may have to install blocking between the rafter and the ceiling joists.

For the gable ends, you will have to stud-in the area between the rafters. This is simply a matter of cutting two-by-fours and installing them vertically, on 16-inch centers. The studs will attach to the top plate and to the bottom of the rafters.

The last step in the roof framing is the collar ties. Collar ties are usually made from two-by-sixes or two-by-eights. They are just short pieces of wood that are nailed between two rafters to tie them together. Each pair of rafters should be connected with a collar tie.

INSTALLING THE NEW SHEATHING

With your framing done, you are ready to begin installing the new sheathing. CDX plywood is normally used for roof sheathing, but particle board is an alternative material that is used in many parts of the country. Since roof sheathing is not normally a tongue-and-groove material, plywood clips should be used where the sheathing comes together. These H-clips help to maintain the rigidity of the sheathing. The clips should be installed at the center-point between rafters or trusses.

INSTALLING THE ROOF COVERING

The next step is installing the roof covering. Roofing felt is often applied over the roof sheathing, before shingles are applied. However, some regions favor omitting the felt and applying the shingles directly to the sheathing. I don't recommend roofing without a layer of felt. Omitting the felt may void the warranty on your shingles.

Roof flashing and metal drip edge is generally installed next. Then, the shingles are applied. There is an art to running shingles. With proper planning and the use of chalk lines, you can get an even and attractive roof. A square of shingles is the equivalent of 100 square feet. The starter course of shingles will usually extend about one-half of one inch over the drip edge. The edges of the roof will normally have a shingle exposure of about five inches.

FIGURE 2-3
A creative conversion. *(Courtesy of National Gypsum.)*

TRADE TIP

Roofing felt is often applied over the roof sheathing, before shingles are applied. However, some regions favor omitting the felt and applying the shingles directly to the sheathing. I don't recommend roofing without a layer of felt. Omitting the felt may void the warranty on your shingle.

If you use roofing nails to attach your shingles, you should use four nails, with a length of one-and-one-quarter inch, in each strip of shingles. If you use a pneumatic stapler, the staples should have a wide crown and should be one-and-five-eighth inches long. Make sure your nails or staples penetrate thoroughly and allow the shingles to lay flat.

When your roof flashing, drip edge, and shingles are installed, you have completed the roofing part of your project.

Raising your roof can make quite a difference in the appearance of your home. Not only will raising the roof make a visual difference, it will allow more space for living. In some cases you will have enough room to install a kitchen, for independent living, in the conversion project.

3

Framing Floors, Walls, Ceilings, and Partitions

In any type of conversion project, you are likely to have to deal with framing walls, ceilings, or partitions. Framing is not particularly difficult, but doing it right isn't as easy as some people think. This chapter is going to show you various ways to deal with the framing of your walls, ceilings, and partitions.

Are you wondering what the difference is between a wall and a partition? If so, let me shed some light on the subject. Partitions are generally considered to be interior walls that separate two areas, usually two rooms. Walls are most often thought of as the exterior framing and load-bearing framing in a building. You would be correct to call either of these framing structures walls. However, the trade usually defines them as exterior walls, load-bearing walls, and interior partitions.

FRAMING EXTERIOR WALLS

Framing exterior walls might be required in either an attic conversion or a garage conversion. There are many methods that could be employed to accomplish this goal, but there is one way that seems to be used by professionals on a regular basis.

TRADE TIP

Cold weather makes working with air-powered tools more difficult. If the air compressor is set outside, in cold temperatures, special procedures are needed. For example, additives must be provided to the compressor to keep the air from turning into condensation and freezing.

Most professionals build exterior walls and then stand them up and put them into place. This is the first procedure we will explore.

PRE-FAB YOUR WALLS

When you are building exterior walls, you can usually pre-fab them. This process allows you to frame the entire wall under comfortable circumstances. The framing is usually done on the sub-floor of the structure you are building. Let me explain how this is done.

First, lay out the locations for all of your exterior walls. This is usually done by marking the sub-floor with a chalk line. Once you have your lay-out marked, measure the length of your bottom plate. If you are dealing with a long span, you may want to build your wall in sections.

Cut your bottom and top plates to the desired length. If you are building with a standard ceiling height, you can use two-by-four studs that are pre-cut to the proper height. If you are working to a unique ceiling height, cut you wall studs. Remember to allow for the thickness of your top and bottom plates. Most carpenters use one two-by-four as a bottom plate and install two two-by-fours for the top plate.

Once all of your pieces are cut, you are ready to pre-fab your wall. Turn the bottom and top plates over onto their edges. Place your first stud at one end of the plates and nail it into place. Next, do the same with a second stud, at the other end. Many pros use air-powered nailing guns, but a regular hammer will get the job done. Once your two ends are nailed, check to make sure your framework is square. Then, proceed to

PRO POINTER

Pre-fab walls can fall over when workers stand them up. Bracing should be installed to prevent this from happening. While this is not such a big deal on interior partitions, it can be a major safety issue on exterior walls.

install the remainder of your studs. Wall studs are typically installed with a distance of 16 inches between them, from center to center. You should use two nails in each end of your studs.

When your wall section is complete, you are ready to put it into place. If you are working with a large wall section, you may need some help in standing it up and getting it into place. Some carpenters just stand the walls up and nail them in place. Others take time to place wood blocks on the band board as a safety feature. By taking two-by-fours, about 18 inches long, and nailing them to the band board, so they stick up past the sub-floor, it gives you a bumper to butt your wall section into. This bumper makes it easier for a small crew to stand up large walls and it reduces the risk of the wall section falling off the framing platform.

Another step to take before standing up your wall is the installation of prop braces. These prop braces are nothing more than long two-by-fours nailed on the ends of the wall section. These braces will hold the wall up, once it is standing. You will also need some blocks of wood to nail in behind the braces, where they rest on the sub-floor. With large wall sections, you should prepare braces in the middle of the wall, and possibly at intervals between the center and end braces.

Once the wall is standing, position the braces to support the wall. The end of the brace should be sitting on the sub-floor. Nail a block of wood to the sub-floor to prevent the brace from moving. Next, nail the bottom plate to the sub-floor and floor joists. That is all there is to building a pre-fab wall section.

PRE-FAB KNEE-WALLS

When you want to pre-fab knee-walls, the procedure is a little different. Knee-walls are meant to sit on a flat sub-floor and to tie into the rafters above. This means that the top plate for a knee-wall will not be flat, like with a normal exterior wall. The top plate must be angled to fit the pitch of the roof rafters. There are two common ways of building this type of wall on the floor.

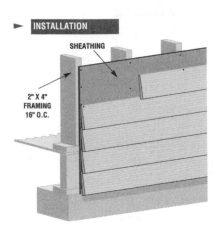

▶ INSTALLATION

VINYL, WOOD, CLAPBOARD SIDING
Apply horizontal siding directly over the sheathing. Fasteners should have a 1" penetration into each framing member. Butt siding joints over framing members.

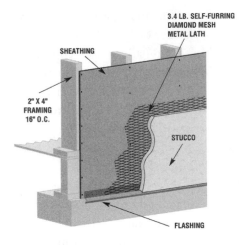

STUCCO
Nail 3.4 lb. Self-furring Galvanized Diamond Mesh metal lath through the sheathing into the framing.

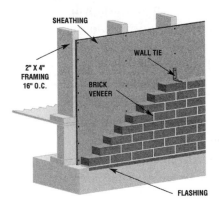

BRICK VENEER
Wall ties for masonry veneer should be nailed through the sheathing with nails that penetrate a minimum of 1" into the framing. Leave an air space of 2" between sheathing and veneer.

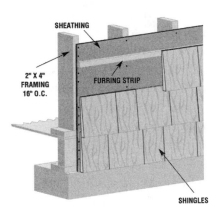

SHINGLES OR SHAKES
Apply 1 x 2 wood furring strips horizontally over the Gypsum Sheathing, spaced to correspond to the shingle exposure, using nails of sufficient length to provide at least 1" penetration into the studs. Nail furring through the sheathing into the framing with a minimum of one nail at each intersection of stud and furring.

FIGURE 3-1
Sheathing facts. *(Courtesy of National Gypsum.)*

You can cut your wall studs on an angle that will allow the top plate to be in alignment with the rafters. In doing this, the pre-fab procedure is about the same as described earlier. Cut your top and bottom plates. Figure the angle needed for the wall studs and cut them. Then, nail the section together. From there, you simply stand the wall up and nail it to the rafters, sub-floor, and floor joists. Remember to check your wall alignment before nailing it into place permanently.

The other way of doing this doesn't use a traditional top plate. First, cut your bottom plate and tack it into position. Then, using a plumb bob or a stud and a level, mark the bottom plate for proper stud placement. Keep in mind that, for this type of framing, your studs will be nailed into the sides of the rafters. Therefore, when marking your bottom plate, you must have your stud located so it will stand next to a rafter.

When you have marked all the stud locations on the bottom plate, remove the plate from the sub-floor. Cut your studs so that they will be long enough to reach from the bottom plate to a point above the rafter, allowing the stud to be nailed to the rafter.

Nail the studs to the plate, just as you would in any pre-fab situation. Next, stand the wall up and get it in the desired position. Check alignment and nail the bottom plate in place. Then, nail the studs to the rafters, but check each stud with a level as you go. It is easy for this type of wall to get out of square while you are working with it.

When the wall is secure, cut two-by-four blocking to install between the studs. This blocking will be nailed horizontally between the studs, providing a nailing surface, similar to a top plate. If you don't like cutting angles, this method will work best, but the angled method is the choice of most pros.

TOE-NAIL METHODS

You could use toe-nail methods to frame your wall, but these methods are generally more difficult and not as strong. In the case of building a knee-wall, you could cut each stud on an angle to mate with the rafters. Then, you could nail the stud to the face of the rafter, rather than the side, as described above. On regular walls, you could erect the top and bottom plates and toe-nail the studs between them, but I can't imagine why you would want to.

PARTITIONS

Partitions will be framed with the same basic procedures already described for walls. Partitions are typically held in place with nails driven into floor joists, ceiling joists, and connection points with adjoining walls. These connection points are frequently a place where studs have been doubled up, to allow a better nailing surface for the connection. Some carpenters use wood blocking between the studs of exterior walls to allow a nailing surface for partition walls.

WORKING WITH BASEMENT WALLS

Working with basement walls can offer additional and different challenges. The exterior walls of basements are usually made from concrete or masonry material. The floors in basements and garages are normally concrete. The walls in basements are often uneven. These walls offer little opportunity for insulation. In daylight basements there are generally ledges that run around the entire basement, about four feet above the floor. This ledge is the result of the thick concrete wall giving away to the thinner wood-framed wall of the daylight section. All of these factors call for different techniques.

ATTACHING WALLS TO CONCRETE FLOORS

There are three basic ways to attach wood walls to concrete floors. You can use a drill bit to drill into the concrete. Once the hole is drilled, you can insert a lead of plastic anchor that will accept a screw. This allows you to screw the wall plate to the concrete floor. As the screw goes into the anchor, the anchor expands to hold the screw firmly. This method works, but it is very time consuming.

Concrete nails are another way of attaching your walls to the concrete floor. Safety glasses are a must for this procedure. Nails meant for use with concrete are brittle and frequently break into pieces. When under the impact of a hammer, the nail pieces will go flying into the air. This procedure also works, but there is a better way.

With today's new tools, you can use a powder-actuated device to drive special nails through your wood and into the concrete. These tools can be rented, but smaller versions can be purchased at very reasonable prices. In the smaller version, you insert one of the special nails into the barrel of the device. Then, you put a small, rimfire powder cartridge into the chamber of the tool. You should be wearing gloves, ear protection, and eye protection when using this type of tool. The next step is to place the end of the barrel of the tool where you want the nail to be driven. Then, you hit the top of the tool with a heavy hammer, and boom, your nail is driven.

These tools are great, but they can be dangerous. Read and abide by all of the manufacturer's suggestions in operating these tools and in nail and powder cartridge selection.

FURRING BASEMENT WALLS

If you are not concerned with adding heavy insulation to your existing basement walls, you can use furring strips to prepare the walls for wall coverings. It is a good idea to coat the masonry or concrete walls with a moisture sealant before installing new walls over the existing walls.

Furring strips should be attached to the wall with an adhesive and nails, whenever possible. The same tool used to shoot nails into the floor will work on the walls.

DID YOU KNOW?

With today's new tools, you can use a powder-actuated device to drive special nails through your wood and into the concrete. These tools can be rented, but smaller versions can be purchased at very reasonable prices. In the smaller version, you insert one of the special nails into the barrel of the device. Then, you put a small, rimfire powder cartridge into the chamber of the tool. You should be wearing gloves, ear protection, and eye protection when using this type of tool. The next step is to place the end of the barrel of the tool where you want the nail to be driven. Then, you hit the top of the tool with a heavy hammer, and boom, your nail is driven.

TRADE TIP

When you are attaching wood to concrete floors, it is best to use pressure-treated lumber. The concrete will give off moisture that can be absorbed by regular wood. Over time, this moisture may rot the wood.

If the basement walls are not even, you will have to place shims behind the furring strips. Use your level to determine when the furring strips are in the proper position, and then secure them to the wall.

When you want to add insulation, but don't need a lot, you can use foam boards to insulate between the furring strips. This insulation can be attached to the basement walls with an adhesive.

BUILDING FALSE WALLS

When existing basement walls are way out of plumb or you need to add heavy insulation, building false walls is your best approach. This is done by framing walls, as mentioned earlier in the chapter, and nailing them to the floor and ceiling joists. This gives you a wall with full depth for insulation, plumbing, wiring, and heat. It also allows you to have a straight and even wall surface.

WORKING WITH LEDGES

In daylight basements, it is common for a ledge to run around the perimeter of the basement. This type of wall problem can be dealt with in two ways. You can frame a new wall between the ledge and ceiling joists to give you a straight, vertical wall. But, if you do this, any existing windows will be set deep into the wall, requiring a window box. Some people like this look and enjoy having the window box to set items in.

If you don't want the window box, you can leave the ledge and trim it out with an attractive trim board. This gives you a finished ledge that can serve to hold everything from collectibles to cocktails. What can you do with your basement? Basements can serve many needs, such as the following:

- An exercise room is a good addition to your basement.
- Use your basement as an office.
- Put a game room in your basement.
- Family rooms are commonly found in finished basements.

CEILINGS

Ceilings are a necessary part of any finished room. You will have different conditions with various types of ceilings. Let's take a look at what you may run into.

GARAGE CEILINGS

You are likely to run into one of two types of situations in framing garage ceilings. In one situation, you will not have any framing to do. This will be the case when you already have ceiling joists, collar ties, or truss bands in place. If you look up in your garage and see framing that will allow you to attach to a flat surface, for a smooth ceiling, you are all set.

If you are converting the lower level of your garage, you should not need to do any additional framing for the ceiling. If you are converting the attic of your garage, you may already have collar ties that will allow the installation of your finished ceiling. If you don't have a flat surface framed up, you can simply nail collar ties across the rafters to make a flat ceiling. This procedure allows for the easy installation of a finished ceiling. You might use drywall, acoustical tiles, or tongue and groove imitation planks.

If you choose ceiling tiles or planks, installation can be easy and quick. You simply nail a metal frame-work to your joists, and hang the ceiling material. Small metal tabs hold the ceiling material in place.

ATTIC CEILINGS

Attic ceilings are like the ceilings in the upper level of garages. If you don't already have suitable framing for a ceiling, adding collar ties will solve your problem. Even if you choose to hang your ceiling to the rafters directly, to create a vaulted ceiling, remember your needs for proper ventilation. It is a wise idea to install collar ties high on the rafters in these cases, to allow a small flat ceiling for ventilation. We will talk about basement ceilings later in this chapter, but I want to tell you how to deal with second-floor joists that you may find in

DID YOU KNOW?

Second-floor joists are the floor joists for the attic and the ceiling joists for the rooms below the attic. The joists in most attics are spaced too far apart to be used as floor joists for living space. These joists are also very often too small to make adequate joists for living space.

garages or attic areas that are too small for your needs before we go into basement conditions.

BEEFING UP SECOND-FLOOR JOISTS

It is necessary with most attic conversions to beef up the second-floor joists. These joists are the floor joists for the attic and the ceiling joists for the rooms below the attic. The joists in most attics are spaced too far apart to be used as floor joists for living space. These joists are also very often too small to make adequate joists for living space. With these two facts in mind, let's see what can be done about the problems.

JOISTS THAT ARE TOO SMALL

PRO POINTER

If the attic floor you are converting into living space is covered with insulation, it should be removed. It may be possible to store the existing insulation for use later in the project.

TRADE TIP

By doubling the width of a joist with a scabbing procedure, you are increasing the strength of the structural member. When allowed, this is a fast and economical way to beef up your floor joists.

It is not uncommon to encounter existing attic joists that are too small for supporting living space. This, however, is not a major problem. For the example that I am about to give you, assume your attic has existing joists that are two-by-sixes, 24 inches on center. Also, remember that any excessive disruption in the attic may cause damage to the ceilings below.

In this example, you are planning to add two bedrooms and a bathroom in your attic space. After checking the local building code, you find that to carry this load, you need floor joists that are

two-by-eights, 16 inches on center.
You presently have two-by-six
joists, 24 inches on center. What
will you do? It's simple; you will
leave the existing joists in place,
and add new two-by-eight joists,
16 inches on center.

However, your job may be
complicated by electrical wires and insulation. Before stocking
your job with lumber, look for existing obstacles that must be dealt
with. If you have electrical wiring running rampant in your attic
floor, you will have to make adjustments before installing new
joists. This may mean only pulling staples and moving the loose
wiring to a more agreeable location, or, you may have to have an
electrician come in to make the needed adjustments.

If the wiring is all run close to the ceiling of the rooms below,
you may be able to use blocking to elevate the new joists above the
wiring, if ceiling-height requirements will allow such a rise. To do
this, you would install blocking, usually two-by-fours laid flat on the
top plate, to set your new joists on. This creates a shallow chase-way
between the new joists and the ceiling below.

The next step is getting your new joist material into the work-
space. The most difficult part of this operation may be getting the
floor joists into the attic. Since you are going to be installing bedrooms in your attic, you will have to install egress windows. This
gives you one option of getting your lumber into the attic without
going through the finished area of your home. If you already have
windows in your gable ends, you can slide the lumber through the
windows. If you don't have windows yet, cut a rough opening for one
of the windows and use the opening to pass the lumber through.

You can construct a sort of plywood sliding board to pull the
lumber up. You could lay an extension ladder up against the house
and use it as a base to hoist the lumber into the attic. If you will be
cutting in a dormer, say for the bathroom, you can bring the lumber
in from the dormer opening. There are many creative ways to get the
new joist material into the attic.

Once the lumber is in the attic, you are ready to install the new joists. Cut the new joists to the proper sizes and set them in place. In most cases you will be using two pieces of wood to span the distance of the attic. One end of each joist will sit on the outside plate. The other end of each joist will rest on a bearing partition or beam. When the two joists meet at the bearing point, the lumber should be long enough for each joist to extend past the other. As these two joists lay next to each other, nail them together. The joists should also be nailed to the top plates and to the bearing wall. Once the joists are nailed in place you, should add blocking between the joists to keep them from twisting.

SCABBING JOISTS TOGETHER

Depending upon your structural requirements, you may be able to get by with scabbing new joists onto your existing joists. As always, check with your local code enforcement office before doing any major work, but this option could save you some time and money. If you are allowed to scab new joists onto the old joists, you will not have as much work to do. This procedure will require existing joists with dimensions of at least two inches by six inches.

Your new joists should be the same size as the existing joists. Place the new joists beside the existing joists, and nail the new joists to the top plate, the bearing wall, and to the existing joists. When nailing the new joists to the old joists, maintain a regular pattern and interval in your nailing. I would recommend nailing at the bottom, in the center, and at the top of each joist, with the horizontal spacing not exceeding 16 inches. You probably don't need this many nails, but the added nailing will reduce the risk of twisting and weakness.

JOISTS THAT ARE TOO FAR APART

Finding joists that are too far apart to support living space is another common problem with attic conversions. Since most attic joists are spaced 24 inches apart and most floor joists for living spaces are spaced 16 inches apart, it is easy to see how this problem arises. Now, let's see how to correct the problem.

If your only problem is needing your joists to be closer together, you can simply add more joists, just as described above.

SHORTENING THE SPAN

There are times when the span of attic joists will create problems with a conversion to living space. Since much of the weight of a roof is supported by the exterior walls, there is not a heavy demand on attic joists for weight support. This can cause a significant problem with attic conversions.

> **DID YOU KNOW?**
> Minimizing ceiling damage during an attic conversion is possible with the use of blocking. By placing blocking under new floor joists, between the joists and the top plates, you keep the new joists from coming into contact with the existing ceiling. This will help to avoid ceiling damage, but it is no guarantee against nail pops and other types of minor damage.

The unsupported span of attic joists will depend on the placement of bearing walls or beams below the joists. It is possible to add bearing walls and beams to increase support and shorten attic spans. However, this will mean remodeling, to some extent, in the home, below the attic.

If you must add support walls or beams, you must have them positioned to rest on a solid foundation. This foundation could be the home's foundation or pier foundations installed just for the new bearing support. In any event, the bearing wall or beam must be supported by a solid foundation of adequate strength for the job.

Once the new bearing wall or beam is installed, the attic joists will have a shorter span between unsupported intervals. This increases the strength of the joists and will solve your problem.

MINIMIZING CEILING DAMAGE

Minimizing ceiling damage during an attic conversion is possible with the use of blocking. By placing blocking under new floor joists,

TRADE TIP

The unsupported span of attic joists will depend on the placement of bearing walls or beams below the joists. It is possible to add bearing walls and beams to increase support and shorten attic spans. However, this will mean remodeling, to some extent, in the home, below the attic.

between the joists and the top plates, you keep the new joists from coming into contact with the existing ceiling. This will help to avoid ceiling damage, but it is no guarantee against nail pops and other types of minor damage.

The downside to blocking under new joists is the loss in ceiling height. Ceiling height is usually at a premium in attic conversions, and blocking can be all it takes to ruin the ceiling requirements. If you want to install your new joists with blocking, you may be able to raise the existing collar ties to pick up some extra height. It may be necessary to use new lumber for the relocated collar ties. Some builders use two-by-fours for this purpose, but I prefer two-by-sixes. When relocating the collar ties, use three 16d nails in each end, in a triangular pattern. There you have it. That should be all you need to know about beefing up your joists for an average attic conversion.

BASEMENT CEILINGS

All basements are equipped with a ceiling structure, but it may not be to your liking. This is especially true if it is littered with pipes, wiring, and duct work, resulting in low head clearance. Let's take a look at how you can work around some of the common problems with basement ceilings.

PIPES

It is not unusual to find pipes running beneath the ceiling joists in unfinished basements. Many homeowners see these pipes and automatically assume they must install a hanging ceiling, to hide the pipes. This is not always the case.

If you are willing to go to the trouble, and expense, most pipes can be relocated and raised to be hidden in the joists. There may be some drain pipes that will not allow this luxury, but most pipes can be raised. If it is not too expensive, it will be worth your while to make the necessary adjustments to allow the installation of a standard ceiling. Real estate appraisers are not kind to cheap, amateur-looking hanging ceilings. However, don't get me wrong, there are some very impressive ceiling options available if the pipes cannot be moved.

WIRES

Wires are frequently stapled to the bottom of the ceiling joists in basements. These wires could be moved into the joists, but there is an easier way to hide them. You can simply drop the ceiling joists down with furring strips. The furring strips will allow a chase-way for the wires, while allowing the installation of a traditional ceiling.

DUCT WORK

Duct work that hangs from basement ceiling joists is not so easy to hide. But, there are ways to improve the look of these metal monsters. If you have duct work, you will have one large trunk line that runs most of the length of your basement. This large duct work must stay below the joists and be boxed in.

The smaller supply and return ducts can usually fit in the space between joists. It may take a little cutting and metal bending, and bleeding, but you can move most of these small ducts. I'm serious about the bleeding, even professionals often cut themselves on the sharp edges of duct work; be careful.

The old holes in the trunk line, from the relocated ducts, can be covered with new sheet metal that is held in place with screws. Before you attempt such a conversion with your heating system, consult with a local expert to be sure you will not harm your heating system.

BEAMS

Beams are a frequent fact of life with basement conversions. They are unwanted, but usually needed. One way to make the most of your beam is to box it in and install recessed lighting in the box, so the box has a purpose, other than just hiding a beam.

You can build your false box around the beam and attach it to the ceiling joists. This allows you to make it any reasonable size that you like. If you prefer to simply wrap the beam, drill holes in the beam with a high-quality drill bit. Wear eye protection and be aware that the metal shavings will be hot. Bolt two-by-fours to the beam and create a box just slightly larger than the beam. Then, you can attach drywall to the wood and cover the beam with a close-fitting box.

▶ DETAILS

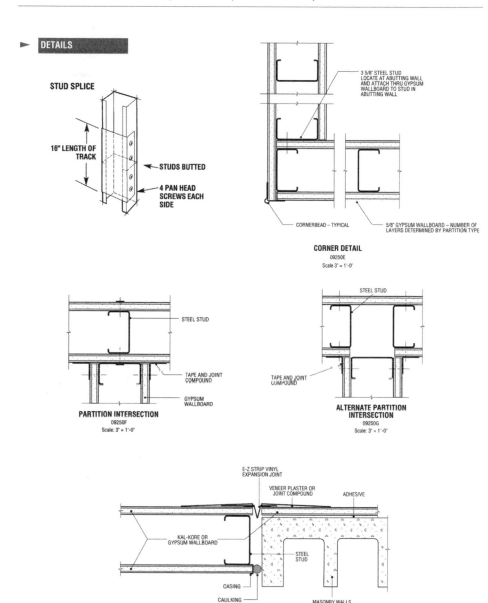

FIGURE 3-2
Framing specifications. *(Courtesy of National Gypsum.)* *(continued on page 42)*

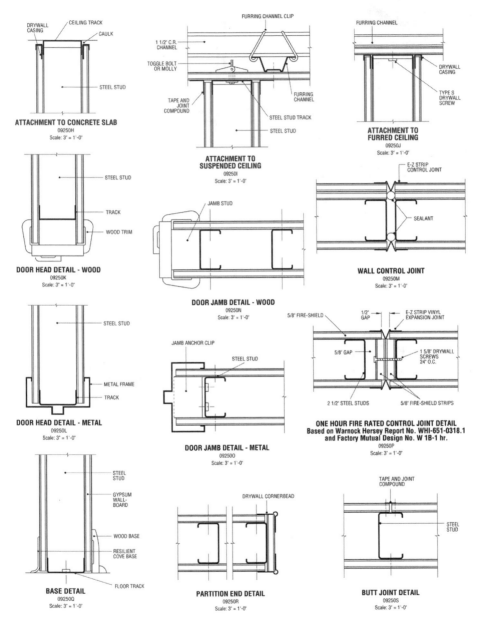

FIGURE 3-2
Framing specifications. *(Courtesy of National Gypsum.) (continued)*

4

Windows, Skylights, and Doors

Windows, skylights, and doors can make the difference between an average conversion and an outstanding showplace. These items can set the pace for an entire habitat. Natural light and good ventilation is critical to pleasant environments. With the proper selection and use of windows, skylights, and doors, your home can become a fantasy getaway.

This chapter is going to show you many of the options available in windows, skylights, and doors. In addition to showing you various product lines, you will be given expert advice on when and where to use the various options. Further, you will be given detailed information on the qualities to look for in your purchases. This valuable information will help you to find your way through the maze of products on the market, to the windows, skylights, and doors that are best for you.

WINDOWS

Windows are not what they used to be. No, they are no longer just simple pieces of glass held in place by small pieces of wood. Today's windows offer features that can save you money on fuel bills. They are designed to make cleaning easy. You can have windows that push up, roll out, or tilt in. There are even windows that don't require painting, and that's not all. Let's take a tour of the windows you can choose from for your conversion project.

CASEMENT WINDOWS

Casement windows are known for their energy-efficient qualities. These fine windows are easy to clean from inside the home, and they offer the advantage of full air flow. When you crank out a casement window, the entire window opens. If you want to smell sea breezes or the fresh morning dew, casement windows open the world to your senses.

These practical, yet attractive, windows can be used in almost any application. You can build a picture-window setting with them. You can frame a bay window with them and build in a window seat to enjoy the view and open air. Decorative transoms can be installed above casement windows to add a touch of elegance. The options for these windows are nearly endless.

> **? DID YOU KNOW?**
> Casement windows are known for their energy-efficient qualities. These fine windows are easy to clean from inside the home, and they offer the advantage of full air flow.

DOUBLE-HUNG WINDOWS

Double-hung windows are the workhorses of the industry. These perennial windows have endured the test of time. But today, the double-hung window has taken on new qualities. These qualities include tilting sashes and removable grids, for easy cleaning, along with high efficiency ratings for minimum heat loss. Add to this vinyl cladding, for low maintenance, and you have a window that is afford-able and consistent in an ever-changing world.

OCTAGONAL WINDOWS

Octagonal windows are ideal for bathrooms and stairways. These appealing windows are available with glass that opens or that remains fixed. The glass selections allow for numerous designs and colors. Your imagination can run wild with these handy windows that can shed light on the smallest of areas.

> **PRO POINTER**
> Octagonal windows are ideal for bathrooms and stairways. These appealing windows are available with glass that opens or that remains fixed. The glass selections allow for numerous designs and colors.

FIGURE 4-1
An unusual window treatment. *(Courtesy of National Gypsum.)*

AWNING WINDOWS

Awning windows can set your home apart from the crowd. These windows open out and up, allowing air circulation, even during gentle rains. When closed, these windows, if grouped together, form a wall of glass. Due to their nature, awning windows can be placed above eye-level, to allow fresh air and privacy, at the same time.

BAY AND BOW WINDOWS

Bay and bow windows are available in pre-made units. Simple to install, these distinctive windows give your new space a new look. With a combination of stationary and movable glass, these window units can be just what your new space needs.

SKYLIGHTS AND ROOF WINDOWS

Skylights are ideal for letting light into your attic conversion. Whether you want a model that opens or one that remains closed, you will have plenty to choose from when you shop for skylights and roof windows.

What is the difference between a skylight and a roof window? In general terms, skylights are mounted in the roof, normally beyond arm's reach. Roof windows, on the other hand, are installed in the side of a roof, to allow views of the grounds and distant scenery. Roof windows are within easy reach and offer many advantages over reg-

---

- The tops of windows should be set at 80 inches.
- Sill heights for windows adjacent to counters should be at least 42 inches.
- Sill heights for windows near furniture should be at least 42 inches.
- Sill heights for picture windows should not exceed 38 inches.

FIGURE 4-2
Suggested window measurements.

ular windows and dormers built only to provide light. Let's see how these interesting roof windows might fit into your plans.

ROOF WINDOWS

Roof windows are an excellent choice for attic conversions. These special windows let in a lot of light, yet they can be equipped with window treatments to control the lighting. These windows are available in a multitude of sizes, for any need. They are easier to install than a gable dormer, and they allow for broader views and more light. Here are some advantages of roof windows to consider:

> **DID YOU KNOW?**
> Skylights are ideal for letting light into your attic conversion. Whether you want a model that opens or one that remains closed, you will have plenty to choose from when you shop for skylights and roof windows.

FIGURE 4-3
An elegant window design. *(Courtesy of National Gypsum.)*

- These versatile windows can be purchased to swing out or tilt in.

- Some models rotate to facilitate cleaning.

- Used in a bathroom, the large operable area vents the bathroom and removes moisture quickly.

- There are models available that are sized to meet the requirements for emergency egress, when used in a bedroom.

- Most roof windows are available with screens, so you can enjoy the open air without insect infestation.

- All and all, roof windows deserve a serious look for your attic conversion plans.

SKYLIGHTS

Skylights have matured since the days of the plexiglass bubble that sat on top of contemporary homes. These bubbles are still available, and they are a very affordable way to brighten an attic conversion, but now, the sky is the limit for skylight options.

Modern skylights open, have built in shades available, and can be equipped with screens. They are also available with insulation features not found in older skylights. There are even control options available that will close the skylight for you if it starts to rain. With some units, you can use a keypad to control the window treatments and the opening and closing of the glass. Further, there are special rods, some are even motorized, that allow you to operate out-of-reach skylights.

EXTERIOR DOORS

When you begin to look at the options for exterior doors, they may stagger you. Not only can you choose from wood, metal, glass, and fiberglass, the myriad of styles and designs could fill a book. Here, we will look at some of the types and designs that might work best in your conversion remodeling.

STANDARD ENTRY DOORS

Standard entry doors are doors that are normally three feet wide and that hinge on one side. Aside from this generic description, the options available in entry doors are enormous.

> **TRADE TIP**
>
> When deciding on what type of door you want, remember that wood doors may require more maintenance than other types of doors, such as steel or fiberglass.

METAL INSULATED DOORS

For the price, metal insulated doors are a good choice for most applications. These doors are available as solid doors, solid doors stamped to give the appearance of a six-panel door, and with half of the door being glass, with or without grids. Metal insulated doors are very affordable and perform well.

WOOD DOORS

Wood doors are capable of providing beauty not found in other types of doors. The carvings and designs on these doors range from modest to the ornate. Wood doors generally cost more that metal insulated doors, but they do offer looks that are not possible with a metal door. Further, wood doors can be stained and metal doors cannot.

However, wood does have its drawbacks. The insulation quality of a wood door will not match that of an insulated door. Wood doors are also subject to swelling in damp weather. This can cause problems with the doors sticking or not latching properly.

FIBERGLASS DOORS

Fiberglass doors are available in a host of designs. Some brands can even be stained. These doors provide a good wood-look-alike appearance without the swelling problems and with better insulation qualities.

GLASS DOORS

Glass doors are available in various types of frame materials. These doors allow light to flood the interior, but lack in insulation and security qualities.

DOORS FOR THE DECK OR PATIO

Doors for the deck or patio may play an important role in your conversion if you will be adding a balcony or deck to your newly converted space.

FRENCH DOORS

French doors have enjoyed a reputation of prestige for many years. These doors are filled with glass and separated by grills. Both panels of a double French door open. These doors can get very expensive, but they give a distinguishing look.

GLIDERS AND SLIDERS

Sliding glass doors have long been known as sliders or a patio door. Sliders are still available, and they are an appropriate choice in some circumstances. As with most products, the quality of these doors makes a big difference in how well they work.

In upper-end doors, there are gliders. These doors are constructed of high-quality materials and with different techniques from those used in the common slider. Gliders also offer more aesthetic options.

HINGED PATIO DOORS

Known by many names, the hinged patio door is a double-door unit where only one panel opens. The second panel is fixed and remains sealed at all times. These doors have gained popularity with their energy efficiency and ease of operation.

Now that you have an idea of the types of windows, skylights, and doors that are available to you, let's take a look at some of the technical aspects you should look for in your selection.

TECHNICAL CONSIDERATIONS

When you shop for windows, skylights, and doors, there are some technical questions you may want to ask. The following section will get you started on the road to asking the right questions:

- If the unit you are buying will be installed in a location where it could be broken and cut occupants of the home, tempered glass should be installed in the unit.

- The R-value is a rating assigned to identify the resistance a material has to heat flow. The higher the R-value, the better insulated the unit is.

- U-value is not as well known as R-value. U-value is a rating assigned to determine the total heat flow through a unit. A unit with a low U-value has better insulating qualities than a unit with a higher U value.

- The UV-blockage rating of a unit indicates the amount of reduction in ultraviolet rays passing through the unit. The higher the UV-blockage rating, the better.

There are other considerations to appraise when comparing units. However, most of these considerations are a matter of taste and money. By looking at cut-away sections and product information, it will be fairly easy to compare products. Each brand will boast its own special features. It will be up to you to decide what features you are willing to pay for.

THE INSTALLATION OF YOUR UNITS

The installation of your units will depend largely on the type of unit you purchase. For specific installation instructions, refer to and follow the manufacturer's suggested installation methods. With there being so many possibilities for different products, it is not feasible for me to give you precise installation instructions on these items. I will, however, show you the basics.

FRAMING FOR WINDOWS

Framing for windows is not difficult once you know what size to make the rough opening. When you decide what style, type, and brand of window you will be using, you can get the rough-opening dimension from your supplier. The rough opening-dimension will be larger than the actual window.

When framing for a window, you will frame an opening in the wall with the use of jack studs, cripple studs, and a header. The header may be made from lumber nailed together, or nailed with spacers between the boards, to make up the proper width. The jack studs will be installed under the header to hold it up. The jack studs are nailed to standard wall studs and the header rests on the tops of the jack studs. The header is nailed to the wall studs.

A horizontal board is installed below the header, at a distance equal to the rough-opening dimension. This board is nailed to the wall studs and is supported with, and nailed to, short studs from below. The area above the header is filled with cripple studs. These cripples extend from the header to the top plate, completing the window frame.

FRAMING FOR EXTERIOR DOORS

Framing for exterior doors is similar to framing windows. Most doors are available as pre-hung units. This means they come to the site ready to set into the framed opening. When this is the case, framing a door is done with the same procedure used to frame a window, with one exception. The rough door opening should extend all the way to the sub-floor. The header, jack studs, and upper cripples will be installed the same as with a window. But, the lower framing done with a window is eliminated, and the section of the bottom wall plate that runs through the door opening is cut out.

FRAMING FOR SKYLIGHTS

Framing for skylights is usually very easy. Most skylights are made to fit between a pair of rafters. In some cases, all you have to do is nail two boards between the rafters to form a box for the skylight. If the skylight is extra large, you may have to head off a rafter and frame out a box.

If you head off a rafter, the first step is cutting the rafter. Once the rafter has a section cut out of it, you nail a board between the two closest rafters, not counting the one you cut. This board should be of the same dimension as the rafters and it should butt flush with the rafter you cut. Nail the board to the two intact rafters, first. Then, place a joist hanger under the cut rafter and nail the joist hanger to your header board. Repeat this process for the other cut-end of the rafter.

When complete, you have a large opening. The next step is to frame this large opening into a size that is right for your skylight. This is often done by framing a box between the rafters and headers.

INSTALLING WINDOWS

The methods used for installing windows will vary, but most windows are easy to install. If your rough opening is plumb and the right size, your windows should be a breeze to put in. Assuming your windows have a nailing flange, and most do, sit the window in the rough opening and make sure it is plumb. Then, nail the window in place by driving nails through the flange. The flange should be on the exterior side of the house.

INSTALLING DOORS

The procedure for installing doors is a little more difficult, but it still is not bad. Set the pre-hung door unit in place. Level it and place shims between the framed opening and the jamb as needed. When the door is plumb, nail the jamb to the framed opening.

SKYLIGHT INSTALLATION

Skylight installation is normally a matter of placing the skylight in the opening, from the outside, and nailing the nailing flange to the framing members. Some types of skylights will have molded nailing flanges that are designed to sit down over the edge of a two-by-four. With this type, your framing must include a raised rim for the skylight to sit on. Once the skylight is situated on the raised box, nails will be driven through the flange and into the box material.

FLASHING

Flashing is what keeps water from leaking past your installation. Many units come with their flashing material already in place, but some don't. Be sure the proper flashing exists or is installed with your unit.

TRADE TIP
Flashing is what keeps water from leaking past your installation. Many units come with their flashing material already in place, but some don't. Be sure the proper flashing exists or is installed with your unit.

As a reminder, remember to follow the manufacturer's suggestions in the installation of your units. It is a good idea to familiarize yourself with the installation recommendations provided by manufacturers to make sure that your contractors are doing the work in compliance with the required procedures.

5

The Stairway

When choosing a stairway design for your conversion project, you should consider all of the options. Some types of stairs are more attractive than others. Certain types of stairs are more practical. Stair design can hinder furniture movement. Code requirements are another factor when debating a stairway choice. This chapter is going to address the issue of stairs. It will show you the most commonly used stairs and some exotic options. In addition, you will learn about code considerations, framing methods, and railing designs.

CHOOSING A STAIR DESIGN

Choosing a stair design is an aspect of your job that deserves deliberate attention. Whether you are descending to a basement family room or ascending to an attic getaway, your stairs will be used time and time again. The wrong design can be frustrating, fatiguing, or even dangerous. Let's take a look at some of the options available to you.

STRAIGHT STAIRS

Straight stairs are just as their name implies, straight. These are the most common, and the most economical stairs. However, this design can be steep and fatiguing, as well as boring.

STAIRS WITH WINDERS

Stairs with winders are not uncommon. This stair design can be installed in a shorter area than a set of straight stairs. The winders provide a place to take a break, relieving fatigue. Stairs with winders can be a simple design, using only a winder at the base of the stairs, or they can be exotic, with many winders and changes in direction.

SPIRAL STAIRS

Spiral stairs are interesting and distinctive. These stairs can be installed with a minimum of space, but many people have trouble navigating spiral stairs. Furniture movement is another problem with spiral stairs. Due to their design, spiral stairs are very difficult to move furniture on. These stairs are fine as a second means of access, but should be avoided as an only means of access, whenever possible.

SWEEPING STAIRS

Sweeping stairs seem to roll downward in a regal fashion. These curving stairs flow like a gentle river, meandering to their destination. This design is impressive, but expensive. Not only is the stair construction expensive, the wall construction needed to follow the curving design adds extra costs.

OPEN-TREAD STAIRS

Open-tread stairs are good for maintaining an open, spacious feeling about a room, but they can be dangerous. Some people have trouble with these stairs because of the open design. By not have a toe-kick, people occasionally miss their footing and fall.

FIGURE 5-1
The curve of the staircase adds to the style of the room.
(Courtesy of National Gypsum.)

RAILING OPTIONS

Railing options go on and on. You can opt for a conservative railing, or you can spend thousands of dollars on an artistic railing ensemble. The first consideration in railing will depend on your choice in the construction of your stairway. If, for example, you have stairs that are enclosed on both sides by walls, you can choose an inexpensive handrail. When the stairs are open on both sides, you must install a railing assembly of both sides. Some of your railing options are listed below.

BASIC HANDRAIL

The basic handrail is a straight piece of finished wood that attaches to a wall with brackets. The handrail may be round or it may be shaped into a design.

HANDRAILS USED WITH BALUSTERS

The handrails used with balusters tend to be much more expensive. These handrails are typically much larger and more ornate. Component parts are used in conjunction with these handrails to create an attractive assembly. The component parts and balusters used with this type of rail can be costly, but you have numerous options in designing the look you like.

HALF-WALL RAILS

Half-wall rails are often used on the open side of stairs. When one side of the stairs is protected by a full wall, a half wall is often built on the unprotected side. This wall is built at the height required by local codes for a handrail, and is capped with a finished trim board. This type of stair protection is cost effective and offers good protection for small children.

CODE CONSIDERATIONS

Code considerations must be taken into account when building your stairs. Since local codes vary, it will be necessary for you to check with your local code enforcement authorities before building your stairs. I can't tell you what your local code requirements are, but I can tell you the important questions to ask. These questions are as follows:

- What is the maximum riser height?
- What is the minimum stair width?
- What is the minimum tread depth?
- What is the minimum width between handrails?
- What is the minimum clearance requirement for headroom?
- How high should the handrail be?
- How many handrails are required?
- How much space is allowed between balusters?
- How deep should platforms be?

FRAMING FOR YOUR STAIRS

The framing for your stairs will depend on local codes and the type of stairs you are building or installing. Spiral stairs come ready to set into your framed opening. Finished wood stairs are available in pre-fab sets. You might be framing rough steps that will be covered with carpet. If you are installing a pre-fab set-up, frame according to the manufacturer's suggestions. If you are building your own steps, follow the guidelines of your local building code.

> **PRO POINTER**
> Designing, measuring, cutting, and building stairs can be a complicated task. It is generally best to leave this work to seasoned professionals.

FRAMING STRAIGHT STAIRS

Framing straight stairs requires thought, but it is a task that people with some carpentry skills can accomplish. The first part of this job is picking the location for your stairs. Ideally, this should be a place where the stairs will run with the floor joists. If the stairs will be installed to run perpendicular to the floor joists, there will be much extra work involved.

Once you have chosen your location, you must make the rough opening for your stairs. This will involve cutting existing floor joists. The floor joists you cut must be headed off. If you are forced to cut many joists, it may be necessary to add some type of temporary support below the joists. It may also be necessary to install a permanent support below the altered joists.

When you have your rough opening framed in, you are ready to lay out the stairs. Measure the vertical distance between the two floors, where the stairs will be going. Your measurements should allow for the thickness of the finished floor covering. When you have this measurement, divide it by the height you plan to make each riser. For example, if you are going to have seven-inch risers, divide your vertical measurement by seven. This will tell you how many steps you will have.

When you design your stairs, it is important to reach a good ratio between riser height and tread width. When you combine the height of a riser with the width of a tread, the total of the two numbers should be around17½ inches. A typical design might be seven-inch risers and a 10½-inch treads. The combination can work in many variations, as long as you stay within code requirements. You could have a seven-and-one-half-inch riser and a 10-inch tread. The 17½ inch figure is not carved in stone, but it is a good number to work toward.

TRADE TIP

When you design your stairs, it is important to reach a good ratio between riser height and tread width. When you combine the height of a riser with the width of a tread, the total of the two numbers should be around 17½ inches.

When building the stairs, a two-by-four spacer is usually installed on the stud wall for the stair stringer to attach to. This makes hanging drywall easier and reduces air flow that might be a factor in a fire. The two-by-four is nailed to the wall studs at the same angle used by the stringer. Another two-by-four should be

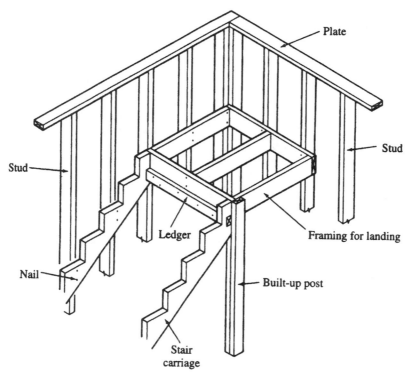

FIGURE 5-2
Typical stair framing.

installed in front of the stringers. This two-by-four is called a cleat, and it provides a place for the stringers to attach to the sub-floor.

Stair stringers or carriages are normally made with two-by-twelve lumber. A framing square is used to draw out the lines for cutting out the riser spaces. Put the framing square on the stringer board with the short arm of the square hitting the top of the board at the desired riser height. Angle the square until the long arm reaches a point equal to the tread dimension. Mark these locations by tracing

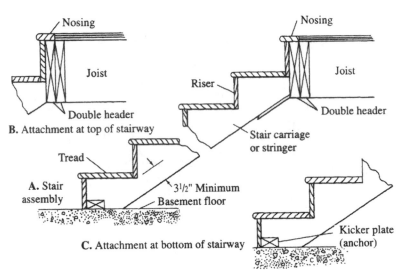

FIGURE 5-3
Attachment at bottom of stairway.

along the square. Continue this process, with the square intersecting with each previous mark, until all riser cuts are marked.

You will want to trim the thickness of a single tread from the bottom of the stringer. You will also need to notch the bottom of the stringer to sit on the cleat or kicker plate. The top of the stringer will need to be notched to sit on a ledger or in a joist hanger. You can nail a ledger to the stairway header for the stringers to rest on, or you can use metal joist hangers to support the stringers.

When you have finished cutting your first stringer, test it to see if your measurements are correct. If they are, use the stringer you have already cut as a template to cut the other stringers. Most stairways should have three stringers, one on each end and one in the middle. After the stringers are

DID YOU KNOW?
Most stairways should have three stringers, one on each end and one in the middle.

installed, you are ready to put the risers and treads in place. Install the risers first and the treads last.

ADDING WINDERS

If you will be adding winders to your stairs, treat each winder platform as a different floor level. Compute your stair from the platform to the finished floor. If your stair design gets too complicated, don't hesitate to call a professional. Many experienced carpenters have trouble with complicated stairs, so be sure to find someone with the skills you require.

OUTSIDE STAIRS

When garage attics are converted to living space, the stairs to the new space are sometimes installed along the outside wall of the garage. This saves space in the building, but it can hurt the appraised value of your improvement. It is best to build your stairs within the structure. Another problem with exterior stairs is exposure to the elements. Climbing outside stairs on snowy or icy nights is dangerous. Whenever possible, keep your stairs within the building.

6

Adding a Dormer

A dding a dormer is a good way to expand an attic and let more light into the space. Dormers can be used to create space for bedrooms, bathrooms, or just for windows. Adding a dormer is a rather large undertaking, but it is a manageable project for homeowners with mechanical abilities. If you need more usable floor space in your attic, a dormer might be your best option.

There are two basic types of dormers. A gable dormer is used primarily to provide space for a window. This type of dormer is particularly popular on Cape Cod style homes. Roof windows may be a better alternative for this purpose, if your only goal is to achieve better light and ventilation in your attic conversion. However, many people prefer the appearance of gable dormers over that of roof windows.

The other type of dormer is a shed dormer. Some people call these dormers strip dormers. The dormers are typically much larger than gable dormers and are used to add more floor space, with better headroom. Small shed dormers are often added to house a bathroom. Large shed dormers can run the length of the attic to expand the whole area.

Installing either of these dormers will mean altering the existing roof. If you have a truss roof, don't try to cut in a dormer. As you learned earlier, engineered trusses are not meant to be cut. If you have a stick-built roof, dormers are a viable option. Let's move ahead and see how to go about building a dormer.

BUILDING A GABLE DORMER

We are going to start with building a gable dormer. Once you know where you want your dormer, you are ready to begin. Make sure the ground around your work area is clear of property and people that may be damaged or hurt from falling objects. Start by removing the roof covering from the area to be occupied by the dormer. You may go ahead with the removal of the roof sheathing once the shingles are out of the way, but don't cut the rafters yet.

Before you cut out the rafter sections you need to place temporary bracing under the parts of the rafters that will be left. This means putting a brace down low, near the top plate of the house and up high, a little above where the rafters will be cut. You can build your braces from two-by-fours in the same way you would pre-fib a wall section. Slide the braces under the rafters and tack them in place with nails.

The next step before cutting the rafter sections is to add additional rafters at the edges of where your rough opening will be. Double up the rafters on each side of your proposed hole. The new rafters should extend from the top plate of the house to the ridge board.

Now you are ready to remove the rafter sections. When you cut out the rafter sections you must be careful not to allow them to drop and damage the ceiling below the attic or the side of the house. When you cut the rafter sections, cut them at an angle that will accommodate the new dormer. A bevel gauge is helpful

---

PRO POINTER

Before you cut out the rafter sections to build a dormer, you need to place temporary bracing under the parts of the rafters that will be left. This means putting a brace down low, near the top plate of the house and up high, a little above where the rafters will be cut.

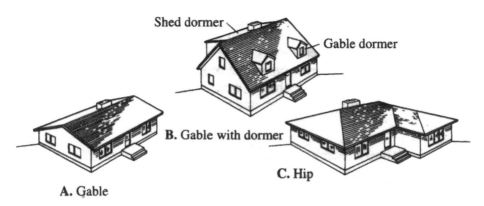

Shed dormer

Gable dormer

B. Gable with dormer

C. Hip

A. Gable

FIGURE 6-1
Roof pitch types.

in obtaining the desired angle. Once you have the rafters cut out, you are ready to install your headers.

With this type of dormer you will have the lower portion of the original rafters remaining; this is where you will put the first header. The header will span across from the two doubled rafters and attach to the lower rafter sections that are left. Use metal joist hangers to attach the rafter sections to the header. Once this header is complete, you will install another header near the ridge pole. This header will span from the two jack rafters and butt against the center rafter that you cut.

Once the headers are installed, the remainder of the job is just basic framing. The side studs for the dormer will sit on the doubled rafters. You will run a ridge board from the front of the dormer to the header you installed near the main ridge board. The ridge board will be supported on the outside end by a stud rising from

DID YOU KNOW?
Framing a shed dormer can be a much bigger job than building a small gable dormer. You are affecting much more of the existing roof structure and the size of the project can be considerably larger.

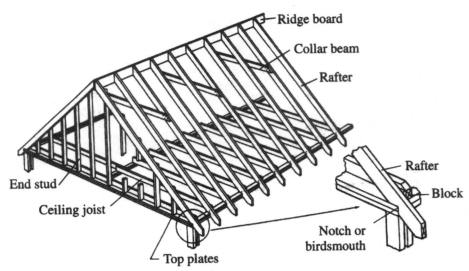

FIGURE 6-2
Typical rafter framing.

a double top plate in the new dormer. The two valley rafters will run from the doubled rafters to the new header you installed near the main ridge board. The jack rafters will connect with the valley rafters and tie in.

The front studs of the dormer will rest on the lower header and extend to the dormer's top plate. The dormer's top plate will attach to the front and side studs. The front gable end of the dormer will be filled in with studs connecting from a double top plate to the dormer's roof rafters and ridge board. The roof of the dormer will be framed with rafters extending from the top plate to the ridge board.

TRADE TIP
When planning the hole for a shed dormer, don't cut too close to the gable ends on the roof. You will want some of the rafters and sheathing to remain on each end.

FRAMING A SHED DORMER

Framing a shed dormer can be a much bigger job than building a small gable dormer. You are affecting much more of the existing roof structure and the size of the project can be considerably larger. The process for framing a shed dormer is different, so let's see how to do it.

OPENING THE ROOF

Opening the roof for a shed dormer will be done nearly the same as with a gable dormer. The only major difference will be that the only rafter sections left will be those attached to the ridge board. Instead of leaving short sections of rafters sitting on the top plate, as dis-

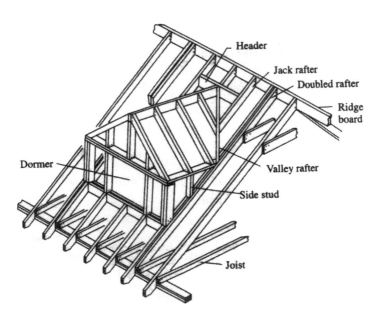

FIGURE 6-3
Gable dormer framing.

cussed for gable dormers, you remove the entire section, so the new dormer can sit on the house's top plate. When planning your hole, don't cut too close to the gable ends on the roof. You will want some of the rafters and sheathing to remain on each end. Once the roof is open, you are ready to begin framing.

HEADING OFF THE SEVERED RAFTERS

Start your framing by heading off the severed rafters. Your header should span the dormer opening and attach to the doubled rafters. Once the header is in, you can begin to frame the dormer walls. The front wall of the dormer is framed like any other wall. It sits on the top plate of the house and its top plate will accept the new rafters for the shed dormer. Remember to brace this wall so that it does not fall off the house. The braces can swing back into the attic and be nailed to blocks attached to the attic's sub-floor.

The next step is installing the new dormer roof rafters. One end of the rafters will attach to the header with joist hangers. The other end will be notched to sit on the top plate of the new dormer. Start by cutting a single rafter. Once you have one rafter with the proper notch and angle, use it as a template for cutting the remaining rafters. Go ahead and install the rafters. Where the rafters sit on the top plate, toe-nail them in.

Now you are ready to install the side-wall studs. The bottom plate for these studs will sit on the existing roof sheathing. Cut the bottom plate and nail it to the existing roof and doubled rafters. Once the plate is secure, you can begin to cut your side-wall studs.

The side-wall studs will normally be notched with an L-shaped notch at the top. This notch allows the stud to cradle the end rafter. Since the bottom plate is installed on a slope, the bottom of the side-wall studs will have angled cuts. The studs will get progressively shorter as they move from the front of the dormer to the back. Nail the studs to the bottom plate and to the end rafters. When this is done, so is your framing.

CLOSING IN THE DORMER

After the framing is done, you are ready to close in the dormer. The roofing methods described in Chapter 2 can be used to install the roof sheathing and shingles. The walls should be covered with some type of sheathing. Some builders use plywood for wall sheathing and others use particle board. Many carpenters use a foam insulation board for sheathing, and some use fiber-board sheathing.

Local codes will probably require wood sheathing on the corners or the use of corner braces, in the absence of wood sheathing. The type of sheathing used will depend upon your preference and local customs.

Of course, you will want to put your windows in before you side the new dormer. Whether you want a gable dormer or a shed dormer you can add a sewing room, bedroom, or family room in your unused attic.

7

Exterior Siding Alterations and Trim

I f you will be adding a dormer or raising your roof, you will have to make alterations and additions to your existing exterior siding and trim. Compared to the job of building the dormer or raising the roof, this job will seem easy.

TYPES OF SIDING

There are several different types of siding. There is wood siding, vinyl siding, hardboard siding, and aluminum siding, to name a few. The types of siding most often used in modern building techniques are wood and vinyl. Some types of siding are installed horizontally and others are installed vertically. Most siding comes in widths of either four or eight inches, but some types of siding come in four-foot-by-eight-foot sheets. Siding is generally sold in quantities called squares. One square is equal to 100 square feet.

EXTERIOR TRIM COMPONENTS

The exterior trim components usually consist of a fascia board and a soffit. To understand the types of exterior trim components, refer to the list below:

- The soffit is the trim you see when you look up, under the overhang.

- The fascia board is the board that conceals the tails of the rafters.

- Frieze boards are the trim boards that are installed at the top of the siding, where the siding meets the soffit.

- Rake boards are boards on the gable ends that run parallel with the roof slope and trim out the side of a home.

DID YOU KNOW?
Siding is generally sold in quantities called squares. One square is equal to 100 square feet.

DIFFERENT METHODS OF INSTALLATION

There are many different methods of installation for the various types of siding. Here are some examples of how different types of siding are installed:

- Vinyl siding is typically installed horizontally. This durable siding is installed with the use of special installation pieces, and each piece of siding overlaps and locks into the previous piece of siding.

- Wood clapboards are thick at the top and narrow at the bottom. This wood siding laps over the previous piece of siding and nails to the exterior wall. Clapboards are installed horizontally.

- The siding that comes in large, four-by-eight panels is normally installed vertically. These panels butt to each other and are nailed to the exterior wall. The seams with these panels are covered by an integral tab on the siding.

- Wide planks are sometimes installed vertically on a house for siding. When this is done, the boards butt together, and the seam is covered with a smaller, vertical trim board.

- Some wood siding comes in long lengths and goes together with a tongue-and-groove method.

- Siding shakes are small, individual pieces of siding that are lapped over each over to cover the exterior of the house.

There are many options on the various types and installation methods of siding.

WORKING WITH WOOD CLAPBOARDS

In many cases you will be working with wood clapboards. When you add siding to cover new framing, matching the old siding and color can be the hardest part of the job. There are two schools of thought here. The first is to match the new with the old as closely as possible. The second is to make the new siding different, so it doesn't look like a failed attempt to match the old siding. Further, if you are siding a small dormer, the dormer should be high enough and far enough away from the old siding that a minor mismatch will not be apparent.

> **TRADE TIP**
> Most of today's wood clapboards are pine or cedar. If you don't know which type of siding you have, take a small sample to your lumber supplier for an evaluation. By using the same species of wood, you can do a good job with custom-mixed paint or stain to match existing siding, even if it has weathered.

In most traditional homes, changing the pattern of the siding or the type of siding will not look good. Contemporary homes allow more freedom for changes in direction and styles of siding. In conversion projects, the new siding being added can almost always be separated from the old siding. Dormers are naturally separated. When raising the roof, the new siding will be on the gable ends. Creative use of trim boards can provide separation for this siding.

WHICH SIDE IS EXPOSED

Homeowners frequently begin their siding job with the question of which side of the siding to leave exposed. Wood siding has a rough side and a smooth side. If you will be painting the siding, install it with the smooth side exposed. When you plan to stain your siding, install the siding with the rough side exposed. Stain soaks into the rough side a lot better, for a deeper coverage.

CORNER BOARDS

Corner boards will be needed on the corners of your framing. These wood strips are installed vertically and give the siding a place to end. Corner boards are normally made of one-inch material. They are

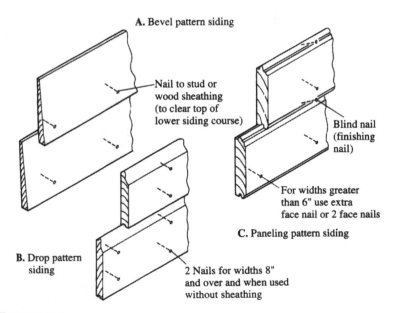

FIGURE 7-1
Methods of nailing wood siding.

installed on each wall at the corner and butt together. Interior corners are made by installing a vertical square wooden strip. This inside corner strip frequently has a dimension of one and one-quarter inches.

HANGING THE SIDING

Hanging the siding requires some planning. All window flashing and other flashing needs should be installed before the siding is applied. The average lap for wood siding should be no less than one inch. A starter strip is nailed at the bottom of the wall to be sided. Local codes will normally require a minimum clearance between the siding and the earth, but in attic conversions, this will not be a factor.

> **TRADE TIP**
> Hanging siding requires some planning. All window flashing and other flashing needs should be installed before the siding is applied.

The thick end of the siding is the bottom. The first piece of siding is placed on the starter strip and nailed in place. Then the next piece of siding is set over the previously installed piece and nailed into place. The siding nails should be going into wall studs. Many carpenters mark the exterior walls with chalk lines to keep the siding even and in good appearance. Without the chalk lines, it is easy to have the siding stray and end up with mismatched exposure.

> **DID YOU KNOW?**
> When trying to match new vinyl siding with existing vinyl siding, you must take into account how much the existing siding has faded over time. The best way to do this is to take a sample of the existing siding to a supplier and use it to determine what the best shade of new siding will be for your home.

VINYL SIDING

Vinyl siding has become very popular and is found on many houses. This siding is durable and never needs painting. Due to its nature, vinyl siding expands and contracts. This expansion and contraction requires special installation methods. If the siding is not installed properly, the expansion and contraction can damage the siding.

NAILS

The nails used to install vinyl siding should be either galvanized steel or aluminum roofing nails. The head of the nail should be about three-eighth of an inch. Each nail's shank should have a diameter of about one-eighth of an inch. The length of the nail will be determined by the thickness of materials to be nailed through. The nails should be long enough to penetrate at least three-quarters of an inch into a stud.

DID YOU KNOW?
You should never nail into the face of vinyl siding. The siding will have a nailing strip; this is where the nails belong. It is important to place the nails in the center of the nailing slot.

TRADE TIP
When nails are driven into the nail slots, a small gap should be left between the nail head and the slot. If the nail is driven into the slot tightly, expansion and contraction can cause problems.

PRO POINTER
Choose your siding nails carefully. Nails that are too large will split your siding. The wrong nails will rust and send dark stains running down the exterior of your new siding. The proper nails will usually be either aluminum, stainless steel, or galvanized steel.

You should never nail into the face of vinyl siding. The siding will have a nailing strip; this is where the nails belong. It is important to place the nails in the center of the nailing slot. If the nail is too far to one side of the slot, expansion and contraction will be restricted. If the nailing slot does not line up with a stud, you should extend the size of the slot. There is a special tool, called a nail-slot punch that can be used to extend the nailing slot.

When nails are driven into the nail slots, a small gap should be left between the nail head and the slot. If the nail is driven into the slot tightly, expansion and contraction can cause problems. All nails should be driven in straight. If the nail enters at an angle, it can cause stress on the siding. Vinyl siding should never be stretched to fit. If the siding is too tight, problems will arise.

STARTER STRIPS

Starter strips are accessory pieces used to hang vinyl siding. These strips will be installed at the lowest point on the area to be sided. The top of the starter strip will normally be about one and one-half inches above the bottom of the wall sheathing. These strips must be level. Normally, a chalk line is used to mark a level line on the wall sheathing. The chalk line is used as reference point when installing the starter strips.

When starter strips butt together, there should be a quarter-inch gap between the strips. This gap allows for siding movement during expansion and contraction. The same nailing techniques used for vinyl siding should be used for accessory pieces.

> **PRO POINTER**
>
> Avoid butt seams whenever possible. When seams must be made in long runs, stagger the seams. Staggered seams are much more attractive than a uniform line running up the side of your home. Seams should be made at stud locations, so that the end of each piece of siding can be nailed to the stud.

CORNERS

Inside and outside corners are made with corner posts. These posts are installed vertically and extend about one-quarter of an inch below the starter strips. Inside and outside corner posts can be overlapped when additional length is needed. This requires cutting about one inch off of the bottom of the top post. Then, the top post can slide down over the lower post to meld together. The overlap of the post should be about three-quarters of an inch, with one-quarter of an inch allowed for expansion and contraction.

CHANNEL

J-Channel is another accessory piece. J-Channel is used around windows, doors, and at other places to give the vinyl siding something to attach to. It is common to wrap J-Channel all the way around windows to get a finished look. When doing this, another accessory piece, called an undersill, is used for a more professional looking job.

Material	Care	Life, yr	Cost
Aluminum	None	30	Medium
Hardboard	Paint Stain	30	Low
Horizontal wood	Paint Stain None	50+	Medium to high
Plywood	Paint Stain	20	Low
Shingles	Stain None	50+	High
Stucco	None	50+	Low to medium
Vertical wood	Paint Stain None	50+	Medium
Vinyl	None	30	Low

FIGURE 7-2
Siding comparisons.

Some windows come with J-Channel already installed on the window frame.

CUTTING VINYL SIDING

Cutting vinyl siding is not difficult. You can use a power saw with a fine-tooth blade. You could also use a hack saw to cut your siding. Aviation snips also work well when cutting vinyl siding.

HANGING THE SIDING

Hanging the siding is simple. Starting at one corner, usually a rear corner, snap the bottom of the siding into the starter strip. When the siding is seated into the starter strip, nail the siding to the wall studs.

The siding should be held away from the corner posts by about one-quarter of an inch.

When two pieces of siding butt together, the overlap should be between one and one and one-quarter inches. Where these overlaps occur, nails should be at least ten inches away from the overlap. This will make for a neater job. Overlaps should be staggered, to avoid routine seams on the home.

Material	Advantages	Disadvantages
Aluminum	Ease of installation over existing sidings Fire resistant	Susceptibility to denting, rattling in wind
Hardboard	Low cost Fast installation	Susceptibility to moisture in some
Horizontal wood	Good looks If of high quality	Slow installation Moisture/paint problems
Plywood	Low cost Fast installation	Short life Susceptibility to moisture in some
Shingles	Good looks Long life Low maintenance	Slow installation
Stucco	Long life Good looks in SW Low maintenance	Susceptibility to moisture
Vertical wood	Fast installation	Barn look if not of highest quality Moisture/paint problems
Vinyl	Low cost Ease of installation over existing siding	Fading of bright colors No fire resistance

FIGURE 7-3
Siding advantages and disadvantages.

GETTING TO THE TOP

When you are getting to the top of your wall, you should install undersill strips. These finish strips will be installed horizontally, along where the wall meets the roof structure. The last piece of siding to be installed will generally have to be cut. This means cutting off the nailing flange. With the nailing flange gone, how will you attach the siding? You will use a snap-lock punch.

Once you have the top piece of siding cut, use a snap-lock punch to dimple the siding. The dimples should be about six inches apart, and they should be raised on the outside of the siding. When you are done punching the siding, install the bottom of the siding, just as you have been doing all along. Now, instead of nailing the top of the siding, push the dimpled siding into the undersill trim. The raised bumps will catch and hold the siding in place.

Type	Use
Softwood veneer	Cross laminated plies or veneers—Sheathing, general construction and industrial use, etc.
Hardwood veneer	Cross laminated plies with hardwood face and back veneer—Furniture and cabinet work, etc.
Lumbercore plywood	Two face veneers and two crossband plies with an inner core of lumber strips—Desk and table tops, etc.
Medium-density overlay (MDO)	Exterior plywood with resin and fiber veneer—Signs, soffits, etc.
High-density overlay (HDO)	Tougher than MDO—Concrete forms, workbench tops, etc.
Plywood siding	T-111 and other textures used as one step sheathing and siding where codes allow.

FIGURE 7-4
Types and uses of plywood.

GABLE ENDS

Gable ends are finished off with J-Channel. J-Channel is run with the slope of the roof. The siding is cut with the proper angle to allow it to fit into the J-Channel. The J-Channel provides a finished surface and trim to hide the cut edges of the siding.

HELPFUL HINTS

Here are some helpful hints for working with existing siding:

- It is not uncommon for bees to take up residency behind siding.

- Bats have even been known to come flying out from behind old siding as the siding was being removed. When you are up on a ladder and bees or bats suddenly fly out from behind the siding you are working with, you can lose your composure, and your balance.

- Always wear the proper safety equipment.

- Never drop items to the ground without making sure the area below you is clear of people and pets.

Siding is usually one of the easier parts of a conversion project. With the right professionals doing the work, you should see good results in a short period of time. Tackling this type of work on your own will be more of a challenge, but now you know the basics of how to install siding and how to see that your contractors are doing the job properly.

8

Plumbing

Plumbing is one area of work that many people fear the most. This fear is due largely to a poor understanding of how plumbing works. For most residential conversions, the plumbing involved is basic and fairly simple. Many times, the hardest part of the job is finding a way to get new plumbing to the space being remodeled. This chapter is going to give you some insight into plumbing and how you can make your job go a little easier.

TYPES OF DRAIN AND VENT PIPES

There are many types of drain and vent pipes, but there are only a few that you are likely to work with. Let's look at each type.

CAST-IRON PIPE

Cast-iron pipe has long been a workhorse in the plumbing field. This durable pipe has been used for drains and vents for many years, and it is still used today.

TRADE TIP

Let me give you a word of caution. If you are cutting a vertical cast-iron pipe, you should take some extra safety precautions. Cast iron is heavy. When you cut a section out of a vertical pipe, the pipe over your head could come crashing down on you. Always support the pipe sections that might fall on you. You can support these sections with wood braces or with perforated galvanized strapping. However you do it, make sure that the pipe will not come falling down when it is cut.

If you will be remodeling an older home, it is very likely you will have to work with some cast-iron pipe. This is not to say you must run your new plumbing with cast-iron pipe, but you may have to connect your new piping to old cast iron.

In the old days, cast-iron joints were made with oakum and molten lead. Today, there are special rubber adapters available for making connections with cast iron. These rubber adapters slide over the ends of two pipes and are held in place with stainless-steel clamps. Not only is this type of connection much easier to make, it is also safer than working with hot lead.

Cutting cast-iron can be easy, or it can seem like torture, it all depends upon how you do it. If you will be cutting cast-iron pipe, you will do well to rent a rachet-type soil-pipe cutter. These handy devices have a chain that you wrap around the pipe. When the chain is in place, you crank up and down on the handle of the tool. In a matter of moments, the cast iron is cut. Most tool rental centers rent these cutters at very affordable rates.

Let me give you a word of caution. If you are cutting a vertical cast-iron pipe, you should take some extra safety precautions. Cast iron is heavy. When you cut a section out of a vertical pipe, the pipe over your head could come crashing down on you. Always support the pipe sections that might fall on you. You can support these sections with wood braces or with perforated galvanized strapping. However you do it, make sure that the pipe will not come falling down when it is cut.

GALVANIZED STEEL PIPE

Galvanized steel pipe is another old-timer that is still in use. It is not installed much anymore, but there is still plenty of it around. If you have to tie into a galvanized pipe, the cut can be made with a hack saw. The joint can be made with the same rubber adapters used with cast-iron pipe.

PRO POINTER

When you encounter galvanized steel pipe being used for either a drain or for water piping, it is best to replace it. This type of pipe rusts and tends to clog. Whenever feasible, replace galvanized pipe with a more modern type of pipe.

DWV COPPER

DWV copper can still be found as a drain-waste-and-vent (DWV) pipe in older homes. This pipe enjoys a long life and is a good DWV pipe. When you need to adapt plastic pipe to copper, you can do so with rubber adapters. DWV copper can be cut with a hack saw, but a set of copper roller-cutters will do a neater job. Either tool will cut the pipe satisfactorily for use with rubber adapters.

SCHEDULE FORTY PLASTIC PIPE

Schedule forty plastic pipe is the drain and vent pipe most often used in modern plumbing systems. There are two types of schedule forty plastic pipe. The two types are ABS and PVC. ABS is a black plastic pipe. This pipe is easy to cut with a hack saw or hand saw, and it is a breeze to work with. PVC is also able to be cut with a hack saw or a hand saw, but it

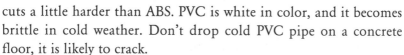

TRADE TIP

Don't drop cold PVC pipe on a concrete floor, it is likely to crack.

cuts a little harder than ABS. PVC is white in color, and it becomes brittle in cold weather. Don't drop cold PVC pipe on a concrete floor, it is likely to crack.

When you are working with these plastic pipes, joints are made with a solvent or glue. With PVC, a cleaner is recommended and a primer is required by most plumbing codes. The cleaner and primer are used prior to gluing the joints together. These types of pipes can be installed with cast-iron or galvanized steel pipe by using the universal rubber adapters.

Abbreviation	Meaning
ABS	Acrylonitrile-butadiene-styrene
AGA	American Gas Association
AWWA	American Water Works Association
BOCA	Building Officials Conference of America
B&S	Bell and spigot (cast iron pipe)
BT	Bathtub
C-to-C	Center-to-Center
CI	Cast iron
CISP	Cast iron soil pipe
CISPI	Cast Iron Soil Pipe Institute
CO	Clean out
CPVC	Cholorinated polyvinyl chloride
CW	Cold water
DF	Drinking fountain
DWG	Drawing
DWV	Drainage, waste, and vent system
EWC	Electric water cooler
FG	Finish grade
FPT	Female pipe thread
FS	Federal specifications
FTG	Fitting
FU	Fixture unit
GALV	Galvanized
GPD	Gallons per day
GPM	Gallons per minute
HWH	Hot water heater
ID	Inside diameter
IPS	Iron pipe size
KS	Kitchen sink
LAV	Lavatory
LT	Laundry tray
MAX	Maximum
MCA	Mechanical Contractors Association
MGD	Million gallons per day
MI	Malleable iron
MIN (min.)	Minute or minimum
MPT	Male pipe thread
MS	Mild steel
M Type	Lightest type of rigid copper pipe

FIGURE 8-1
Commonly used abbreviations. (*continued on page 89*)

Abbreviation	Meaning
NAPHCC	National Association of Plumbing, Heating, and Cooling Contractors
NBFU	National Board of Fire Underwriters
NBS	National Bureau of Standards
NPS	Nominal pipe size
NFPA	National Fire Protection Association
OC	On center
OD	Outside diameter
SAN	Sanitary
SHWR	Shower
SV	Service
S & W	Soil and waste
SS	Service sink
STD. (std.)	Standard
VAN	Vanity
VTR	Vent through roof
W	Waste
WC	Water closet
WH	Wall hydrant
WM	Washing machine
XH	Extra heavy

FIGURE 8-1
Commonly used abbreviations. *(continued)*

TYPES OF WATER PIPE

Many types of water pipe are available. Some are easier to work with than others. Some require soldering skills and others are glued together. Let's see what your options are for water pipe.

COPPER

Copper water pipe and tubing is a long-time favorite for conveying water. This pipe is best cut with roller-type cutters, but it can also be cut with a hack saw. The biggest drawback to copper for homeowners is the need for soldering skills. The normal method for making joints with copper requires the installer to solder the joints. Since many homeowners don't know how to solder, especially when a little water is trapped in the pipe, they opt for another type of pipe.

Even when you run a different type of pipe for the new plumbing, you may have to connect to the existing copper. This can be done, even if you can't solder. Compression fittings can be used to make your transition from copper to the new pipe material. Threaded fittings and adapters can also be used in some circumstances.

CPVC PIPE

CPVC pipe is affectionately referred to within the plumbing trade as the homeowner's friend. Most professional plumbers don't use CPVC pipe. Compared to other options, this pipe is slow and finicky to install for a professional. However, many homeowners find CPVC to be an ideal choice for water pipe.

CPVC is a plastic pipe. It can be cut with a hack saw, and it glues together. A cleaner and primer should be used on the joints before they are glued together. It is important to not move fresh joints. It takes time for these joints to cure. If CPVC is moved before the joint sets up, leaks will occur.

> **DID YOU KNOW?**
> CPVC is a plastic pipe. It can be cut with a hack saw, and it glues together. A cleaner and primer should be used on the joints before they are glued together. It is important to not move fresh joints. It takes time for these joints to cure. If CPVC is moved, before the joint sets up, leaks will occur.

PEX PIPE

PEX pipe is catching on in a big way with professional plumbers. This plastic pipe is very flexible and easy to install with the proper tools. This pipe uses insert fittings and special crimp rings to make its joints. Some types of PEX use thermal expansion and contraction to make joints. The tools needed to make either of these joints can often be rented. They are a necessity when working with PEX and they are substantially expensive, so renting them is the best option.

The pipe can be cut with a hack saw, but special PEX cutters are available.

Due to its flexibility, PEX pipe and tubing can be snaked through walls, much like electrical wiring. Since it is available in long coils, the pipe can be run with a minimum of concealed joints. This fact gives PEX pipe another advantage. For attic conversions, where the pipe must be snaked up, PEX is a good choice. If you decide to use PEX, make sure you have the proper tools and follow the manufacturer's installation procedures.

> **DID YOU KNOW?**
> Due to its flexibility, PEX pipe and tubing can be snaked through walls, much like electrical wiring. Since it is available in long coils, the pipe can be run with a minimum of concealed joints. This fact gives PEX pipe another advantage. For attic conversions, where the pipe must be snaked up, PEX is a good choice.

COMMON ROUGH-IN DIMENSIONS

Let me give you some common rough-in dimensions for various residential plumbing fixtures. The drain for a lavatory should be roughed-in at the center of the lavatory and about 17 inches above the sub-floor. The water pipes for a lavatory will rough-in on four-inch centers, about two inches on either side of the drain, and about 21 inches off the sub-floor.

The drain for a common toilet will rough in 12½ inches of the back stud wall. When measuring from the center of the toilet drain to either side, you should have a minimum of 15 inches of clear space. This means the closet flange should have at least 15 inches from its center to any finished side wall or fixture. The water supply for a toilet is roughed-in six inches to the left of the center of the drain and about six inches above the sub-floor.

A bathtub drain will typically be located 15 inches off the stud wall where the back of the tub will rest. The drain will normally be about four inches off the head wall, where the faucets will go. When roughing in a tub hole, most plumbers cut the hole to extend from the head wall to a point about 12 inches away and about eight inches wide. This gives you a hole that is eight inches wide and 12 inches long. You will need most of this space to connect a tub waste and overflow to the tub.

If you are installing a faucet for a tub, the faucet is usually set about 12 inches above the flood-level rim of the tub. The flood-level rim is the arm rest or location where water will first spill over the tub. The tub spout is normally mounted about four inches above the flood-level rim of the tub.

When installing the faucet for a shower, the faucet is ordinarily set about four feet above the sub-floor. The shower head outlet should be installed about six feet and six inches above the sub-floor.

The drains for a kitchen sink will set between 15 and 18 inches off the sub-floor. The water supplies for a kitchen sink are normally roughed-in about 21 inches above the sub-floor.

A washing machine hook-up will have a standpipe that extends between 18 and 30 inches above its trap. The water supplies will be set at a height in the neighborhood of four to five feet above the floor.

With all fixtures, hot water should be piped to the left side of the fixture and cold water should be piped to the right side of the fixture.

All of these dimensions are averages and will vary with local plumbing codes and specific product manufacturers. Check product information and local codes before installing your plumbing.

BASEMENT PLUMBING

Basement plumbing can present its own set of challenges. The drains may be too high to allow new fixtures to drain by gravity. It can be quite difficult to get a vent pipe from the basement to the roof. The concrete floor might need to be broken up to install plumbing. The list for possible complications goes on. Let's see how to deal with some typical basement plumbing problems.

HOW CAN I FIND THE DRAINS UNDER MY FLOOR?

One way to find drains under your floor is to look for clean-out caps. These screw-in caps are installed to allow access for cleaning the drain lines and they provide a visible means of locating some pipes. You could start breaking up the floor at the base of plumbing stacks entering the floor. This way is effective, but it can cause undue damage to the floor. If your drains are made from cast iron, a good metal detector can be used to trace the direction of your under-floor drains.

THERE AREN'T ANY DRAINS UNDER MY FLOOR, WHAT CAN I DO?

If you are installing a toilet, you will need to install a sewer ejector or a specialty toilet. Some toilets are designed to flush up, others incinerate waste. If you are only installing a sink, like for a wet bar, you

FIGURE 8-2
A basement installation would be perfect for this luxurious bathroom. *(Courtesy of American Standard.)*

may be able to tie into an existing pipe, before it exits the foundation. If all the pipes are above your drainage level, you will have to install a pump.

Installing a sewer ejector is not a complicated job, but it does require a bit of labor. The concrete floor must be broken up. A jackhammer, which you can rent, will do a nice job on residential floors. Then, a pit must be dug to accept the sewer pump. Once the sump, a watertight container, is set in place, you run the plumbing beneath your floor. The plumbing fixtures drain into the sump. When the waste level rises to a certain point, the sewer pump will cut on and pump the waste out of the house.

The sewer pump will plug into a normal household electrical outlet. The sump will have a gasket-sealed top and will be vented to the outside air to avoid odors and sewer gas from entering the basement. The drain pipe from the pump will have a check valve to keep the waste in the vertical piping from running back into the sump. There will be a gate valve installed on the drainage line to facilitate repairs and maintenance on the pump.

The concrete floor will need to be filled in and patched. The filling in is usually done with sand. The patching is usually done with a sand mix, similar to concrete, but without the rocks. The sand mix is easier to float out for a smooth finish.

HOW DO I VENT MY PLUMBING?

Under most plumbing codes, every plumbing fixture must have a vent. There are many ways to vent a plumbing fixture, but the most common is with an individual vent that runs to a vent stack or outside air. Vents must rise at least six inches above the flood-level rim of a fixture before being run horizontally.

In some cases, a kind plumbing inspector may allow the use of a mechanical vent. These vents screw into a one-and-one-half-inch female adapter and provide air for a fixture to drain better. In remodeling jobs, these vents are sometimes allowed in lieu of running a vent all the way to the roof. However, if you are installing a toilet or a sewer sump, plan on running a two-inch vent to the outside air or to an approved connection point with another vent.

> **TRADE TIP**
> If you live in a cold climate, try to avoid installing plumbing vents on the outside of your home. While this is generally legal, you must prevent the vent from freezing. During cold weather, condensation will occur in the pipe and freeze. Install an oversized pipe if you must run an exterior vent to reduce the risk of the pipe closing up due to ice buildup.

When you have to get a vent from your basement to your attic, look for closets to run the vent in. Consider building a small box-chase in a corner to allow the installation of the pipe. The routing of the vent from a basement is often the hardest part of the job.

CAN I RUN MY VENT UP THE OUTSIDE OF MY HOUSE?

Some plumbing codes do allow side-wall vents. These vents must be protected from freezing, in cold climates, and they must not terminate under a soffit vent. There are restrictions pertaining to the proximity of the vent to windows, doors, and even property boundaries. Check with your local code officer for details on side-wall vents.

MY DRAIN GOES OUT AT FLOOR LEVEL, WHAT CAN I DO?

If you position your bathroom or plumbing near the existing drain, you may be able to build up the new floor, with a sleeper system, to allow height for your new drains. Check your ceiling height requirements before raising the finished floor level.

CAN I TIE INTO THE PIPE FOR MY FLOOR DRAIN?

Most floor drains will be connected to a pipe of at least two inches in diameter. In fact, the minimum pipe size for pipes running under concrete is usually two inches. The floor drain could be connected to a three- or four-inch drain.

As long as you vent your new fixtures, there shouldn't be any problem with tying into the same drain used by your floor drain. The plumbing code does set requirements for the number of fixture-units placed on a pipe, so check with your local requirements before making such a connection. For example, you would not be able to install a toilet and have its drain tie into a two-inch pipe. The minimum pipe size for a toilet drain is three inches.

> **DID YOU KNOW?**
> New plumbing installations require a permit from the local plumbing inspector. If you are adding plumbing to a house that you live in, you can obtain the permit as the homeowner if you are going to do the work yourself. Otherwise, the permit must be obtained by a licensed, master plumber.

CAN I CUT A TEE INTO THAT VERTICAL PIPE FOR MY LAVATORY?

The odds are good that you can cut a tee into the vertical pipe for the lavatory. The pipe must have a minimum diameter of 1¼ inches, but almost any plumbing pipe you encounter will be at least this large.

CAN I TIE INTO MY KITCHEN SINK'S WATER PIPES?

It depends on how many fixtures you will be tying into the pipes and how many fixtures are already served by the pipes. As a rule-of-thumb, don't serve more than two plumbing fixtures with ½ inch water line. If the pipes have a ¾ inch diameter, you should be fine.

ATTIC PLUMBING

Attic plumbing can be very different from basement plumbing. For one thing, gravity drainage isn't a problem. Access to vents is not much trouble. However, getting water pipes into the attic can require some thought. Let's take a look at attic plumbing.

FIGURE 8-3
An attic space can make a charming bathroom. *(Courtesy of American Standard.)*

CAN I USE THIS BIG VERTICAL PIPE FOR A DRAIN?

The big vertical pipe extending through the attic is a main vent. Normally, it will be acceptable to tie into this pipe as a drain. However, as with all plumbing, check with your local code officer first.

HOW CAN I GET PLUMBING UP TO MY ATTIC?

To get plumbing up to your attic, you may have to open existing walls from below. It is possible that you can build chases for the pipes to run up, such as in closets. In some cases, it may be possible to snake pipes up through existing partitions. If the walls are not filled with fire-blocking or wiring, it is often possible to get pipes up without opening the walls.

SINCE MY ATTIC PLUMBING IS SO HIGH UP, DOES IT NEED A VENT?

Yes. All plumbing fixtures should be vented.

HOW CAN I GET A BATHTUB INTO MY ATTIC?

One-piece bathtubs cannot be carried up most stairways. If you plan to use a one-piece tub, put it in while you are framing the dormer or attic openings. If this is not possible, opt for a standard bathtub and a fiberglass or tile shower surround or a sectional fiberglass tub-shower combination.

> **TRADE TIP**
> One-piece bathtubs cannot be carried up most stairways. If you plan to use a one-piece tub, put it in while you are framing the dormer or attic openings.

GARAGE PLUMBING

Garage plumbing can offer the difficulty of having plumbing too far away to connect with existing drains. The grade of the pipes may not allow connection. Getting water pipes to the garage can also be a problem. Let's see how to deal with some of these problems.

I WANT A BATHROOM IN MY GARAGE, WHAT SHOULD I DO WITH THE DRAIN?

It may be possible to intersect with your home's sewer at some point in the lawn. If this is not possible, you will have to run a separate sewer for the garage plumbing.

HOW WILL I GET NEW PLUMBING IN MY GARAGE?

You will generally have to break up a section of the concrete floor. This is normally done in a corner. Then, a hole is dug to allow pipes to come in beneath the garage's footing. All pipes coming through or under a wall should pass through a protective sleeve. The sleeve should be at least two pipe-sizes larger than the pipes passing through.

WHEN RUNNING WATER PIPES TO MY GARAGE, HOW DEEP SHOULD THEY BE?

The depth for buried water pipes will depend on the local climate. Your local plumbing code will provide information on the minimum depth to be used when burying water pipes.

HOW MUCH CAN I CUT OUT OF MY FLOOR JOISTS FOR PLUMBING?

Most building codes require a minimum of two inches to be left at the top and bottom of floor joists. Some codes are more lax and require only that one and one-half inch be left at the top and bottom of a joist. If more than this is notched or cut, steel plates or headers are usually required.

HOW OFTEN SHOULD I SUPPORT MY HORIZONTAL PIPES?

The distance between supports will be determined by local plumbing codes and the type of pipe being installed. In general, plan on support intervals of four feet for drain and vent pipes and six feet for water pipes.

IN CLOSING

In closing, I would like to offer some additional advice. Plumbing is a logical trade. With common sense and the right tools, plumbing is not difficult. There are rules to be followed, and you will normally need to apply for a permit to do your work. Most jurisdictions require up to four inspections. If you are running a new sewer or water service, this work will need to be inspected. Any plumbing installed underground or under a floor will need to be inspected before the trench is covered or the floor is poured. All plumbing that will be concealed in walls should be inspected prior to concealment. Finally, after you set your fixtures, a final inspection is par for the course.

Before doing your own plumbing, check with the local code enforcement office for current rules and regulations. Always be sure to have the water shut off to pipes you will be cutting. Avoid contact with the contents of waste and soil pipes. If you are unsure of yourself, call in a professional.

9

Electrical

The task of electrical wiring is underestimated by some and overestimated by others. In logical terms, electrical wiring is not hard to understand. However, working with electricity can be very dangerous. Unlike plumbing, where a mistake is only likely to get you wet, a mistake with electricity can be fatal. While electricity is not to be feared, it is to be respected.

When you convert an attic, garage, or basement to living space, you can count on having to make alterations in the electrical system. You might have to increase the size of the main service panel. You may only have to run a few new circuits or install a ground-fault interceptor, but count on making changes.

UPGRADING A SERVICE PANEL

Upgrading involves working around high voltage, and the risk of a fatal injury is always present. Unless you are a licensed electrician, don't attempt to change your entrance panel.

When will the panel need to be upgraded? Service panels have different ratings, depending upon their size and how they are set up. In old houses, it is not uncommon to find the main electrical panel to be a 60-amp fuse box. These boxes usually have two large, box-like fuses, and a few small screw-in type fuses.

Most modern houses will have circuit breakers in the main service panel. These breaker boxes will usually be rated for either 100 or 200 amps. If your box is set up for 200 amps, it is highly unlikely that you will need to upgrade the panel, unless you have electric heat.

With a sixty-amp fuse box, it would be wise to upgrade to a higher capacity circuit breaker system. If you have a 100 amp service panel and you will be adding electric heat in your converted space, you will want to upgrade to a 200 amp box.

ADDING A SUB-PANEL

Adding a sub-panel can be a big help when wiring for an attic or garage conversion. A sub-panel is essentially a service panel that connects to the main service panel. The sub-panel could contain fuses or circuit breakers, but circuit breakers are the preferred choice of most people.

If you don't install a sub-panel, each circuit in your newly converted space will have to have a wire that runs back to the main service panel. By installing a sub-panel in the vicinity of the new space, you can cut down on the amount of wire used and the number of wires returning to the main service panel. This can save you some money.

When you use a sub-panel, the wires from each new circuit will run to the sub-panel. One large wire will run from the sub-panel to the main service box. It is easy to see how this will save time and wire. Of course, there is the additional cost of the sub-panel, but there is also the convenience and safety of having the panel close at hand.

BOX SELECTION

Electrical box selection is important to the finished job. Depending upon the type of installation you are roughing-in for, you will need the right box for the job. Let's look at some of the options for electrical boxes:

- Rectangular boxes are commonly used for switches, wall outlets, and wall-mounted lights. The dimensions for rectangular boxes are generally three inches by two inches.

Device	Wattage rating
Room air conditioner (7000 BTU)	800
Clothes dryer	5800
Clothes washer	600
Furnace (blower)	1000
Furnace (oil burner)	300
Humidifier	80
Sewing machine	90
Television	120
Vacuum cleaner	650
Water heater	4500
Shallow-well pump	660
Deep-well pump	1320

FIGURE 9-1
Common wattage ratings for general household devices.

- Octagonal boxes are most frequently used for ceiling lights. They may also be used as a junction box to join numerous wires together. These boxes are typically four inches in length along each edge of the box.

- Round boxes are used primarily for ceiling lights.

- Square boxes are most often used as junction boxes. Square boxes have a typical dimension ranging from four inches to just over four and a half inches.

BOX DEPTH

The box depth on electrical boxes varies from one and a quarter inches to a full three and a half inches. This depth plays an important role in determining how many connections the box may hold. For example, a three-by-two switch box with a depth of two and a half inches can accommodate six connections with a number 14 wire. The same box, but with a depth of three and a half inches, could hold nine connections. Ground wires usually count as a connection.

MEANS OF ATTACHMENT

The means of attachment for different boxes will vary, but some ways are easier than others. One of the easiest, and most common, boxes used in modern jobs is the plastic box with nails already inserted. These plastic boxes are nailed directly to wall studs. The boxes are sold with nails already inserted in a nailing sleeve. All you have to do is position the box and drive the nail.

Some metal boxes are set up with a nailing flange that resembles an ear. With these boxes, you position the box and drive nails through the flange, into the stud. This type of box is good because the ear is preset to allow for the thickness of common drywall.

Other metal boxes, usually meant for use in existing construction, are equipped with adjustable tabs. These tabs, or ears as they are sometimes called, allow the box to be attached to plaster lathe, or any other material that will accept and hold screws.

Octagonal and round boxes are often nailed directly to ceiling joists. If these boxes need to be offset, such as in the middle of a joist bay, metal bars can be used to support the boxes. The metal bars are adjustable and will mount between ceiling joists or studs. Once the bar is in place, the box can be mounted to the bar.

TRADE TIP

When you are unable to conceal your wires in a conventional method, wire molding should be used to protect you and the wiring.

COMMON HEIGHTS AND DISTANCES

There are some common heights and distances used in electrical wiring. For example, wall switches are usually mounted about four feet above the finished floor. Wall outlets are normally set between 12 and 18 inches above the floor. Most areas require wall outlets to be spaced so that there is not more than 12 feet between the outlets.

WIRE MOLDING

Wire molding is a protective trim that is placed over wires when the wires are run on the outside of walls and ceilings. This molding can be installed after wiring is run. The wire molding is hollow and open on the bottom; this allows the molding to be laid over existing wires. When you are unable to conceal your wires in a conventional method, wire molding should be used to protect you and the wiring.

DID YOU KNOW?

Color codes are common in wiring. For example, a black or red wire is usually a hot wire. A white wire should be a neutral wire, but don't count on it, these wires can be hot. Green wires and plain copper wires are typically ground wires. When matching these colored wires to the various screws in an electrical connection, they should go something like this. Black wires should connect to brass screws. Red wires should connect to brass or chrome screws. White wires will normally connect to chrome screws. Green wires and plain copper wires should connect to green screws.

Device	Wattage rating
Blender	375
Coffee maker	1000
Dishwasher	1000
Freezer	500
Frying pan	1200
Microwave oven	1200 to 1800
Range	12,000
Refrigerator	350
Toaster oven	1200
Bath fan	100
Hair curler	1200
Hair dryer	1200
Heater	1500
Heat lamp	250

FIGURE 9-2
Common wattage ratings for electrical devices in kitchens and bathrooms.

CONDUIT

Conduit is another option for running wires when conventional methods cannot be employed. However, wires must be pulled through the conduit. Conduit cannot be installed over existing wires. The conduit acts as a protective tunnel for the wires.

SNAKING WIRES

Snaking wires through a wall is done with a fish tape. A fish tape is a thin, flexible, metal tape on a spool. The exposed end of the tape has a hook on it. Some people simply bend the wire to be fished over the hook on the fish tape. Seasoned electricians usually bend the wires over the hook and then tape them, to assure they don't come loose.

Fish tapes can be used to get wires up and down wall cavities. However, fire-blocking in the walls can render a fish tape as being all but useless. It is not unusual for walls to have staggered blocks of wood nailed between the studs. These wood blocks help to block air flow and prevent the wall cavities from acting as chimneys in the event of a fire. If fire-blocking is encountered, the wall must be opened.

Fish tapes are often worked from around outlet boxes. By removing the cover to an outlet box, you have access to the interior of the wall. For example, if you needed a wire in your attic, you could drill a hole in the wall plate. Then, from below, you could remove an outlet cover as the second opening for working the fish tape. Between these two openings, you could fish a wire up or down the wall, to either opening.

COLOR CODES

Color codes are common in wiring. For example, a black or red wire is usually a hot wire. A white wire should be a neutral wire, but don't count on it, these wires can be hot. Green wires and plain copper wires are typically ground wires. When matching these colored wires to the various screws in an electrical connection, they should go something like this. Black wires should connect to brass screws. Red wires should connect to brass or chrome screws. White wires will normally connect to chrome screws. Green wires and plain copper wires should connect to green screws.

PUTTING WIRES UNDER A SCREW

When you are putting wires under a screw, the wire should be bent to tighten as the screw is tightened. If you hook the wire in the opposite direction, it may come loose. Always twist the hook in the end of the wire to go with the clockwise tightening of the screw.

TRADE TIP

When you are putting wires under a screw, the wire should be bent to tighten as the screw is tightened. If you hook the wire in the opposite direction, it may come loose.

Wire color	Status	Connects to
Black	Hot	Darkest screw on device
Red	Hot	Second hot wire in a 240-volt circuit
White	Neutral*	Silver screw on device
Green	Ground	Green screw on device

Note: White wires are sometimes used as additional "hot" wires. Most electricians color the white wire black to indicate this type of use, but don't bet your life on it. Take meter readings on all wires before touching them.

FIGURE 9-3
Color codes used in electrical installations.

Outside dimension (inches)	Wire size #6	Wire size #8	Wire size #10	Wire size #12	Wire size #14
2 × 3 × 2¼		3	4	4	5
2 × 3 × 2½		4	5	5	6
2 × 3 × 2¾		4	5	6	7
2 × 3 × 3½	3	6	7	8	9

FIGURE 9-4
Number of conductors allowed in rectangular boxes.

WIRE NUTS

Wire nuts are available in different sizes and colors. The colors indicate the size of the wire nuts. Wire nuts are plastic on the outside and have wire springs on the inside. When wires are inserted into the wire nut, the nut can be turned clockwise to secure the wires. It may be necessary to twist the wires together before installing the wire nut. It is important to use a wire nut of the proper size. Wire nuts should be installed to a point where no exposed wiring is visible.

SPLIT CIRCUITS

Split circuits are frequently used in kitchens and in rooms where table lights are operated with a switch. In a split circuit, one half

Outside dimension (inches)	Wire size #6	Wire size #8	Wire size #10	Wire size #12	Wire size #14
4 × 1¼		4	5	5	6
2 × 1½		5	6	6	7
2 x 2⅛	4	7	8	9	10

FIGURE 9-5
Number of conductors allowed in round and octagonal boxes.

Outside dimension (inches)	Wire size #6	Wire size #8	Wire size #10	Wire size #12	Wire size #14
4 × 1¼		6	7	8	9
4 × 1½	4	7	8	9	10
4 × 2⅛	6	10	12	13	15
4¹¹⁄₁₆ × 1¹⁄₁₄	5	8	10	11	12
4¹¹⁄₁₆ × 1½	5	9	11	13	14

FIGURE 9-6
Number of conductors allowed in square boxes.

of an outlet remains hot at all times. This is usually the top half of the outlet. The bottom half of the outlet will be controlled by a switch. Split circuits are frequently used in the kitchen to avoid overloading a single circuit. In these applications, it is not uncommon for both halves of the outlet to remain hot, but on separate circuits.

GROUND FAULT INTERRUPTERS

Ground Fault Interrupters (GFIs), sometimes called ground fault interceptors, ground fault breakers, or ground fault outlets are usually required in any location where water may come into contact with the electrical outlet. Bathrooms in particular are generally required to be equipped with a GFI. Outdoor receptacles are another use that normally requires a GFI. Kitchens are also required to be equipped with GFI outlets.

There are two common ways to provide GFI protection. You can install a GFI outlet. These outlets have a test and reset button built into the outlet. It is recommended that GFIs be tested every month. The other manner of protection is a GFI breaker. This is a special circuit breaker that is installed in the service panel. Either of these devices will protect against accidental shocks in a wet area. GFIs are not cheap, but in most areas they are a code requirement for wet-use areas, and they are an excellent safety feature.

DID YOU KNOW?

Bathrooms, kitchens, and outdoor locations for electrical outlets require the use of special ground fault interrupter circuits.

HIGH-VOLTAGE CIRCUITS

Appliances that use high voltage require their own high-voltage circuit. A clothes dryer or an electric range could fall into this category. The outlets for these high-voltage circuits will use a plug with a different pattern from that of a standard wall outlet. Appliances that use these special plugs are often fitted with pigtails. The pigtails are special wiring arrangements, with high-voltage prongs, that allow the appliance to be plugged into the high-voltage outlet. These circuits will run directly from the outlet to the service panel.

FLOOR OUTLETS

Floor outlets are generally frowned upon by electricians and electrical inspectors. When used, electrical outlets mounted in the floor should be equipped with waterproof covers. When possible, avoid installing outlets in the floor.

DESIGN IDEAS

Before we close this chapter, I would like to give you some design ideas for your electrical system. Here are some tips to ponder:

- Ceiling lights are not installed as often as they once were. Some people detest the idea of having a bug-catcher mounted on their ceiling. However, there is still a large portion of the population that likes the idea of having good light cast down from the ceiling. Don't hesitate to install ceiling lights if they suit your fancy.

- Track lighting is popular and can answer many lighting needs.

- Recessed lights can be attractive, but they leave much to be desired in performance. Due to their recessed installation, these lights are limited in the illumination they can provide.

- Lights mounted under the wall cabinets in kitchens have become very popular.

- Exterior motion-sensitive lights are handy, and, if you are converting an attic, it is a good time to have these lights installed in the gable ends.

- Install more outlets and switches than you think you will need. It is much easier to add extra electrical devices while the walls and ceilings are open than it is after the job is done.

- Always apply for the proper permits and have the required inspections on electrical work. Improper wiring can result in personal shocks and house fires.

- Electrical permits are similar to plumbing permits. Homeowners who will be doing their own electrical work in the houses where they live are allowed to apply for their own electrical permit. Otherwise, a licensed electrician must obtain the permit.

- If you hire an electrician, be sure the electrician is licensed and insured.

- Bonding may be another requirement you want to look for in an electrician.

MAKING FINAL CONNECTIONS

I believe that only qualified professionals should make the final connections for electrical wiring. The risk of working inside service boxes and sub-panels is just too great for the average homeowner. I recommend having a licensed electrician look over any electrical work that you do and then have the electrician make the final connections.

10

HVAC

Climate control is a part of any successful remodeling conversion. Heating, ventilation, and air conditioning (HVAC) are all a part of climate control. When you decide to convert unused space into living space, HVAC becomes a factor. Will your existing system be capable of handling the additional load? Should you run a separate zone from your boiler to heat the new space? Would you be better off to install electric baseboard heat in the new living space? Could a wood stove or oil-fired space heater save you money? This chapter will answer these questions and many more you may have about heating and cooling your new habitat.

WINDOW AIR CONDITIONERS

If the climate warrants the use of air conditioning equipment, window air conditioners can be a good choice for converted living space. These independent units are affordable and easy to install. By using a window air conditioner, the

PRO POINTER

The effectiveness of window air conditioners will be determined in part by the design of the living space. If the space is divided into several rooms, a single window unit will not be satisfactory. If, however, the space is mostly open, a window unit can do an excellent job in controlling the climate.

need for additional duct work and the extra strain on an existing central air conditioner is eliminated.

Window units are especially practical when converting a garage. Since garages are usually located far away from existing duct work, it is much easier to install window units than it is to extend new duct work. The amount of livable square footage in a garage is small, when compared to most houses. Because of the smaller habitable space, window air conditioners are quite capable of cooling the area.

In the case of an attic conversion, more than one window unit will normally be required. Since many attic conversions consist of two bedrooms and a bathroom, it would be logical to install a window air conditioner in each bedroom.

CENTRAL AIR CONDITIONING

Central air conditioning relies on duct work to convey its cool air. Since the cool air is dispersed through duct work, the cool air can be directed to all rooms. Central air conditioning provides a more uniform cooling than window air conditioners.

If you plan to extend existing ducts to cool new space, you will

TRADE TIP

Central air conditioning relies on duct work to convey its cool air. Since the cool air is dispersed through duct work, the cool air can be directed to all rooms. Central air conditioning provides a more uniform cooling than window air conditioners.

have to determine if the existing cooling unit is capable of handling the increased load. If the unit is large enough for the job, finding places to run the new ducts will be your next challenge. Ducts are frequently run through built-in chases. It is a simple matter to box in duct work in new construction, but with remodeling work, the task can be more trying.

Consider running the new ducts up through closets. If you need your closet space, find an area that can be boxed in. These areas are often next to closets. When the back wall of a closet extends into a room or hall, there will be a natural chase way created by the wall jutting out. These spaces can be boxed in so that the box becomes an extension of the protruding wall.

FORCED HOT-AIR HEAT

Forced hot-air heat is also conveyed with duct work. The same challenges presented with central air conditioning will exist with forced hot-air heat. Getting the duct work to the desired locations is the most difficult aspect of this type of heat.

When adding forced hot-air heat, keep the registers in the floors or low on the walls. Hot air rises, so the lower the registers are, the more benefit you derive from the heat. Heat registers should be placed along exterior walls, normally around windows.

When using forced hot-air heat, cold-air return ducts should be installed. The number of returns required will depend on the size and design of the converted space. It is generally recommended to install a cold-air return in every large room. The cold-air returns allow cool air to be returned to the furnace for reheating.

HEAT PUMPS

Heat pumps provide heating and air conditioning from a single unit. There are two basic styles of heat pumps. The first type is a through-the-wall heat pump. These units resemble a window air conditioner, in the fact that they are installed through an exterior

> **DID YOU KNOW?**
> One of the drawbacks to a forced hot-air heating system is dust. Since the system works by blowing warm air around the heated space, dust is naturally moved along with the air. For some people, this dust can create uncomfortable living conditions. If you are sensitive to dust, consider a different type of heating.

wall with part of the unit in the home and the other end outside the home. The other type of heat pump has two main parts. There is an indoor part and an outdoor part. The outdoor part sits outside and is connected to the inside part with piping.

Some heat pumps are connected to well systems and are called water-source heat pumps. If you live in an extremely cold climate and want a heat pump, consider a water-source unit. This type of heat pump will be more efficient than a standard, air-source heat pump.

TRADE TIP

Heat pumps are not very efficient for heating when the outside temperature is below freezing. However, most heat pumps are equipped with a type of electric heat to compensate for lower temperatures. While this electric heating will overcome some of the heat pump's heating deficiency, it is an expensive way to heat your home. Heat pumps are ideal in parts of the country where there is a high demand for air conditioning and a low demand for heat.

FORCED HOT-WATER HEAT

Forced hot-water heat is a favorite in cold climates. This type of heating system produces steady heat that can tame the coldest winters. Most modern forced hot-water systems use copper tubing and baseboard heating units. The baseboard heating units contain copper tubing, normally with a three-quarter-inch diameter, that is surrounded by metallic fins. Hot water is forced through the copper tubing and baseboard heating units. Heat is gathered in the fins and radiated into the living space.

This type of heating system depends on a boiler to generate the hot water in the system. The boiler produces hot water, typically with a temperature around 180°F, and a circulating pump forces the water around the heating circuit. It is possible to install multiple zone valves or circulating pumps to create different heating zones. Each zone can be controlled by an independent thermostat. By having individual zones, it is more

PRO POINTER

Forced hot-water heat is a favorite in cold climates. This type of heating system produces steady heat that can tame the coldest winters.

economical to heat a home. Zones serving rooms that are not in use can be turned down, while the heat in active zones is turned up.

If the existing boiler has the capacity to handle new heating demands, new zones can be added to serve newly converted living space. If your existing boiler is old, it might be wise to replace it with a more efficient heating unit. These systems can be installed as a one-pipe system or a two-pipe system. With a one-pipe system, the supply pipe starts at the boiler and makes a continuous loop through the heated area and back to the return side of the boiler. With a two-pipe system, one pipe supplies hot water to the heating units and a second pipe carries the used water back to the boiler.

A one-pipe system is less expensive to install, but it is also less efficient. The water in a one-pipe system cools as it travels through the pipes and heating units. By the time the last heating unit receives its water, the water can be much cooler than when it entered the first heating unit. A two-pipe system provides more stable heat, because the cooled water is returned in one pipe, while hot water is supplied in another.

STEAM HEAT

Steam heat and radiators are found in some older homes. These systems generally work on a gravity principal, without the need of a pump. The piping for a steam system can consist of one or two main pipes. In a one-pipe system, steam rises up the pipe to radiators. As the steam gives off heat, it turns to condensate and runs back down the pipe to the boiler. With a two-pipe system, the steam rises to the radiators in one pipe and the condensate returns to the boiler in another pipe.

Steam heating systems do not respond quickly to temperature changes. This fact alone is

> **DID YOU KNOW?**
> Steam heating systems do not respond quickly to temperature changes. This fact alone is enough to warrant the consideration of a different heating system for your converted space. Further, it is not uncommon for steam heating systems to be noisy. If your present heating system is steam, think about installing a new type of heat in your converted space.

enough to warrant the consideration of a different heating system for your converted space. Further, it is not uncommon for steam heating systems to be noisy. If your present heating system is steam, think about installing a new type of heat in your converted space.

ELECTRIC HEAT

Electric heat can be a good choice for heating converted living space. Sure, everyone is quick to complain about the high cost of operating electric heat, but there are times when electric heat is a reasonable choice.

Trying to run duct work or heat pipes into the attic or garage can be a major chore. At these times, electric heat is something to think about. Electric heat is easy to install and it will provide adequate heat, even if it is expensive to operate. Consider how often you will be heating your new space. The money you save by installing electric heat might go a long way in heating the new space. Before installing electric heat, be sure your electrical panel is large enough. You will probably need a 200 amp panel to run electric heat.

Electric heat comes in many forms. They include the following:

> **PRO POINTER**
>
> Electric heat is easy to install and it will provide adequate heat, even if it is expensive to operate. Consider how often you will be heating your new space. The money you save by installing electric heat might go a long way in heating the new space.

- Most everyone is aware of the baseboard heating units, but they are only the beginning.

- Electric heat can be purchased as a radiant wall heater.

- A fan-forced heater may be your choice of electric heat.

- Register heaters are another option for electric heat.

- How about a kickspace heater? You could install this type of electric heat.

- A hi-wattage wall heater is another option for electric heat.

Remember that hot air rises, and an attic should be warmer than the lower floors of a home. The heat from below will rise to warm the attic if you remove the insulation from the attic floor. Something as simple as cutting a floor register into the attic floor could do wonders for your heating needs. You could cut floor grates in at each end of the attic. These grates will allow even more heat to pass from the downstairs living space to the converted attic.

WOOD STOVES

Wood stoves can add charm and warmth to an area. Combining a wood stove with electric heat is a popular option in some regions. The wood stove provides the bulk of needed heat, and the electric heat provides backup heat and heat for unattended times.

A flue or chimney will be required for a wood stove installation. Most fire codes limit the use of a flue to one connection. Some areas might allow two connections to a common flue, but check local building requirements before tapping into an existing flue. Even if you are allowed to put two connections on a common flue, it is not a good idea. The use of a common flue for multiple connections can lead to excessive soot and creosote build-up. The risk of a chimney fire is increased when more than one connection is made to a common flue. There is also a risk of dangerous gases accumulating, due to poor draft, in an overloaded flue. This can lead to fire or asphyxiation.

Installing a new flue in an attic is fairly easy. A triple-wall stove pipe can be run from the stove to a point above the roof. When installing this metal pipe, follow the manufacturer's installation instructions. When the stove pipe passes through wood, use an approved flange collar to support the pipe and maintain proper dis-

> **PRO POINTER**
> Combining a wood stove with electric heat is a popular option in some regions. The wood stove provides the bulk of needed heat, and the electric heat provides backup heat and heat for unattended times.

> **TRADE TIP**
> Avoid horizontal stove pipe installations. If you must run stove pipe horizontally, keep the horizontal runs as short as possible.

DID YOU KNOW?
Ceiling fans can do a lot to improve the circulation of your heating and cooling efforts. These fans are available with and without light kits. If you have a vaulted ceiling, a ceiling fan is attractive and helpful. If your upstairs will incorporate a loft, a fan with a reversible motor can help maintain a comfortable temperature.

tances from combustible materials. Avoid horizontal stove pipe installations. If you must run stove pipe horizontally, keep the horizontal runs as short as possible.

When picking a spot for your stove, choose a location that will place the stove at least three feet from any combustible material. Even if a wall has a heat shield installed on it, you must maintain a safe distance from the wall. The stove should sit on a fireproof base. This base could be masonry, heavy tile, or stone.

Installing a wood stove in a basement can be more difficult, because of the need to run the chimney. There are two options for installing a metal chimney for a basement wood stove. You can use triple-wall, insulated stove pipe and run it up through the living space of the house until you exit the roof. In doing this, you will most likely want to box in the chimney. This can be done, but maintain minimum distances between the chimney and combustible materials.

Another option is to extend the chimney up the outside of the house. The stove pipe rises from the stove and turns horizontally to exit the basement. When the pipe penetrates the exterior wall, a special adapter should be used to allow the pipe to penetrate the wall without risk of fire. Then, with the use of a wall bracket, the chimney turns to a vertical position and extends past the roof. Stand-off clamps will be installed along the chimney to hold it to the house. By installing the chimney in this fashion, you eliminate the need for disturbing the upstairs living space.

Local building codes will influence the installation of your wood stove and chimney. Chim-

DID YOU KNOW?
If you will be adding a bathroom that will not have a window, you will need a ventilation fan for the bathroom. These fans mount in the ceiling and convey stale air out of the bathroom to the outside air. Many models are available with a built in light.

neys must extend well above the roof. Local codes will dictate the precise measurements for these extensions. As with all remodeling endeavors, check local code requirements before doing your work.

SPACE HEATERS

Space heaters are available in many styles and types. The three most common types are electric space heaters, kerosene heaters, and gas-fired heaters. Space heaters can provide supplemental heat, or even primary heat.

KEROSENE HEATERS

Kerosene heaters require good ventilation. High-quality kerosene heaters are designed to be vented to the outside. These units can be thermostatically controlled and provide good heat. The portable kerosene heaters that are so prevalent do not come equipped with outside vents. These heaters can pose a serious, if not fatal, health risk.

> **PRO POINTER**
> The portable kerosene heaters that are so prevalent do not come equipped with outside vents. These heaters can pose a serious, if not fatal, health risk.

GAS-FIRED HEATERS

Many gas-fired space heaters are designed for a direct vent through an outside wall. These heaters, when properly installed, can provide warmth and comfort, with a minimum of installation aggravation.

ELECTRIC SPACE HEATERS

Electric space heaters do not require a vent. The two possible concerns with this type of heater is the risk of contact burns, which is also present with other types of space heaters, and an overload of the electrical system. Most electric

> **TRADE TIP**
> Before using an electric space heater, be sure the wiring is sized and fused properly.

heaters put a heavy demand on electrical wiring. If your wiring is not up to snuff, a fire could occur. Before using an electric space heater, be sure the wiring is sized and fused properly.

GLOSSARY OF TERMS

AFUE
Annualized Fuel Utilization Efficiency is a measure of your furnace's heating efficiency. The higher the AFUE percentage, the more efficient the furnace. The minimum percentage established by the DOE for furnaces is 78 percent.

Airflow
The distribution or movement of air.

Air Handler/Coil Blower
The indoor part of an air conditioner or heat pump that moves cooled or heated air throughout the ductwork of your home. An air handler is usually a furnace or a blower coil.

Bioaerosols
Microscopic living organisms suspended in the air that grow and multiply in warm, humid places.

Btu
A British thermal unit is a unit of heat energy. One Btu is the amount of heat required to raise one pound of water by one degree Fahrenheit. The higher the Btu rating, the greater the heating capacity of the system.

Btuh
British thermal units per hour.

CAE
The Combined Annual Efficiency is a measure of the amount of heat produced for every dollar of fuel consumed for both home and water heating.

Carbon Monoxide
An odorless, colorless, tasteless, poisonous and flammable gas that is produced when carbon burns with insufficient air.

Central Air Conditioning System
System in which air is treated at a central location and distributed to and from rooms by one or more fans and a series of ducts.

CFM
Stands for Cubic Feet per Minute. This measurement indicates how many cubic feet of air pass by a stationary point in one minute. The higher the number, the more air is being moved through the duct-work by the system.

Compressor
The part of the outdoor air conditioner or heat pump that compresses and pumps refrigerant to meet household cooling requirements.

Condenser Coil
The outdoor portion of an air conditioner or heat pump that either releases or collects heat, depending on the time of the year.

Damper
A movable plate, located in the ductwork, that regulates airflow. Dampers are used to direct air to the areas that need it most. Typically used in a zoning application.

dB
A decibel is a unit used to measure the relative intensity of sound.

DOE
The Department of Energy is a federal agency responsible for setting industry efficiency standards and monitoring the consumption of energy sources.

Ductwork
The method by which air is channeled from the furnace or the blower coil throughout your home.

Electronic Air Cleaner
An electronic device that filters out large particles and bioaerosols in indoor air.

ENERGY STAR®
An EPA (Environmental Protection Agency) designation attached to HVAC products that meet or exceed EPA guidelines for high-efficiency performance above the standard government minimums.

EPA

The Environmental Protection Agency develops and enforces federal environmental regulations. The EPA oversees the nationwide Energy Star® program.

Evaporator Coil

The part of the air conditioner or heat pump that is located inside the air handler or attached to the furnace. Its primary function is to absorb the heat from the air in your house.

Heat Exchanger

Located in the furnace, the heat exchanger transfers heat to the surrounding air, which is then pumped throughout the home.

Heat Pump

A heat pump is an HVAC unit that heats or cools by moving heat. During the winter, a heat pump draws heat from outdoor air and circulates it through your home's air ducts. In the summer, it reverses the process and removes heat from your house and releases it outdoors.

Horizontal Flow

When an air handler or furnace is positioned on its side and circulates air in one end and out the other. Ideal for attic or crawl space installations.

HSPF

The Heating Seasonal Performance Factor is the heating efficiency rating for heat pumps. The higher the rating, the more efficient the heat pump. HSPF will be regulated in 2006 at 7.7.

Humidifier

An indoor air quality device that introduces moisture to heated air as it passes from the furnace into the ductwork for distribution throughout the home.

Humidistat

An automatic device used to maintain humidity at a fixed or adjustable set point.

HVAC

Heating, Ventilation and Air Conditioning.

Indoor Coil

See Evaporator Coil.

ISO 9000
A family of international standards for quality management and assurance.

MERV Rating
The MERV (Minimum Efficiency Reporting Value) rating of a filter describes the size of the holes in the filter that allow air to pass through. The higher the MERV rating, the smaller the holes in the filter and the higher the efficiency.

Micron
A unit of measure equal to one millionth of a meter, or one thousandth of a millimeter.

Odors/Chemicals
Air contaminants in the form of gases.

Outdoor Coil
See Condenser Coil.

Particles
Any substances measuring less than 100 microns in diameter. The EPA has found that small particles (less than 2.5 microns) are responsible for the health effects of greatest concern.

Programmable Thermostat
A thermostat with the ability to record different temperature/time settings for your heating and/or cooling equipment.

R410A Refrigerant
A chlorine-free refrigerant that meets the EPA's newest, most stringent environmental guidelines.

Refrigerant
A chemical that produces a cooling effect while expanding or vaporizing. Most residential air conditioning units contain the standard R-22 refrigerant, or Freon.

Refrigerant Lines
Two copper lines that connect the outdoor air conditioner or heat pump to the indoor evaporator coil.

Scroll Compressor
A specially designed compressor that works in a circular motion, as opposed to an up-and-down piston action.

SEER
The Seasonal Energy Efficiency Ratio is an energy efficiency rating for air conditioners. The higher the SEER, the better the energy performance and the more you save. The DOE's established minimum SEER rating for cooling is 10.00.

Single Package
A heating and cooling system contained in one outdoor unit.

Split System
An HVAC system in which some components are located inside the structure of the house and some are located outside. Split systems should be matched for optimal efficiency.

Thermidistat
Monitors temperature and humidity and adjusts heating or cooling system to maintain desired levels.

Thermostat
Usually found on an inside wall, this device operates as a control to regulate your heating and cooling equipment, allowing you to adjust your home comfort at the touch of a switch.

Ton
Unit of measurement for determining cooling capacity. One ton equals 12,000 Btuh.

Two-Stage Operation
Provides two levels of heating or cooling output for greater temperature control, energy efficiency, and improved indoor air quality.

Upflow
When an air handler or furnace is installed in an upright position and circulates air through the side or bottom and out through the top. Typically used in basement, closet, and attic installations.

Variable Speed Motor
A motor that automatically adjusts the flow of warm or cool air for ultimate comfort.

Ventilator

A system that exchanges stale, recirculated indoor air with fresh, filtered outside air.

Zoning

A method of partitioning a home into independently controlled comfort zones for enhanced comfort and efficiency.

11

Insulation and Drywall

When you get to the insulation and drywall phases, your remodeling job is about half done. Most people consider the worst to be behind them at this stage of the game. However, don't get lulled into a false sense of security. There is still plenty to do and much that could go wrong.

TYPES OF INSULATION

There are several types of insulation to choose from when remodeling your home. Let's examine each of the most common types of insulation and their uses.

BATT INSULATION

Batt insulation is what most people think of when they think of insulation. These batts can consist of glass fibers or mineral wool. Glass-fiber batts are the

DID YOU KNOW?

The thickness of the insulation affects its R-Value. For example, a three-inch batt has an R-value of 11. A six-inch batt has an R-value of 19.

TRADE TIP

When using insulation that is equipped with a vapor barrier, the vapor barrier should be installed so that it is on the heated side of the insulation.

most common. These rolls of batt insulation are available in various thicknesses and R-values.

Batt or blanket insulation is usually available in widths of 16 inches or 24 inches. The 16 inch batts are used between wall studs, and the 24 inch batts are used between ceiling joists. The thickness of this insulation will usually be approximately three inches, six inches, or nine inches. The thickness of the insulation affects its R-Value. For example, a three-inch batt has an R-value of 11. A six-inch batt has an R-value of 19.

Batt insulation is available faced or un-faced. The facing is either a foil or paper backing on the insulation. Insulation installed in walls is usually faced, while insulation in attic floors is usually un-faced. The facing provides a vapor barrier. Batt insulation is commonly stapled to wood studs and joists.

LOOSE-FILL INSULATION

Loose-fill insulation comes in bags and is meant to be spread over an area or blown into an area. The material may consist of cellulose, glass fiber, mineral wool, perlite, or vermiculite. This is the type of insulation frequently blown into existing walls and attics. You can rent machines to blow this insulation into your new attic space. If you buy enough insulation, some stores will loan you the machine for blowing in the insulation.

FOAM INSULATION

Foam insulation doesn't have much of a place in remodeling conversions. This liquid foam can be injected into existing walls with a special machine, but there is little need for it in attic, basement, and garage conversions.

BOARD INSULATION

Rigid board insulation can be used in many ways. It can be installed on a roof to increase the

TRADE TIP

Rigid, board insulation provides a lot of insulating opportunities. The many sizes and uses make this type of insulation a favorite with basement conversions. It can also be very beneficial in attic conversions.

insulating value. It can be installed on basement walls to improve the comfort zone. These rigid boards are sometimes installed below ground, on the outside of basement walls. Foam panels can be used as exterior wall sheathing to increase a home's R-value.

Rigid insulation boards are generally available in widths of 16 inches, 24 inches, and 48 inches. The thickness of these boards can range from a mere half an inch, to a full seven inches.

Rigid insulation may take the form of polystyrene, urethane, or glass fiber. The polystyrene and urethane do a better job than the glass fiber. It is important to install a vapor barrier with polystyrene and urethane boards. Without this vapor barrier, the boards can lose up to half of their R-value to moisture. Board insulation is normally nailed or glued into place.

INSULATION MATERIALS

As you have noticed by now, there are many types of insulation to choose from. There are also numerous types of insulation materials to pick from. What follows is a rundown of the most often used insulation materials and their pros and cons:

- Glass fiber insulation in known for its ability to make people itch. There is also the consideration of breathing in the glass fibers that fly through the air during installation. This insulation is relatively inexpensive, and it is easy, although itchy to install. Glass fiber is good because it does not tend to settle and create voids. Glass fiber is durable and resists most damage that may be caused by water. As a fire risk, glass fiber is low on the list.

- Cellulose is the insulation of recyclers. Cellulose is made from recycled paper. This insulation is inexpensive and easy to install. However, if cellulose gets wet, it loses much of its insulating value. Untreated cellulose presents a high fire risk. If you install cellulose, be sure it has been treated for fire resistance.

- Mineral wool is somewhat similar to glass-fiber insulation. By this, I mean you should take precautions with a mask, gloves, and full body protection when installing it. Like glass fiber, mineral wool can cause irritating reactions in some people.

- Polystyrene is used in rigid boards. This is an excellent insulator, but it is highly flammable.

- Vermiculite is used in loose-fill insulation. This insulator is non-flammable and does not emit any harmful fumes or gases.

- Perlite, like vermiculite, is used in loose-fill insulation. Perlite is non-flammable and emits no harmful fumes or gases.

- Urethane is a name many people recognize as trouble. This insulator was very popular in its foam form. It was used to insulate houses that had no insulation and walls that were difficult to insulate, like brick walls. As time passed, urethane was discovered to offer health hazards, and many locations restricted or banned its use. Urethane is an extremely efficient insulator. However, it is flammable, and when burned, urethane gives off cyanide gas. This deadly gas is one of the primary reasons for some areas restricting the use of urethane.

THE VAPOR BARRIER

Up to this point we have mentioned the vapor barrier, now we are going to see what the vapor barrier is and why it is important.

When insulation is installed in walls and crawlspaces, a vapor barrier should also be installed. If you are using glass-fiber insulation, it can be purchased with a vapor barrier already installed. Another way to create a vapor barrier is to wrap the interior of outside walls with plastic.

When using faced insulation, the facing should be installed to face the heated side of the wall. The goal is to keep moisture from the house from entering the wall cavity. When moisture enters a wall cavity, rot can occur. This is true of walls with no insulation and walls with insulation, but without a vapor barrier.

When the moisture enters the wall, it can attack wall sheathing, insulation, siding, studs, and wall plates. This moisture attack can go unseen for years, until major structural damage has occurred.

WORKING WITH DRYWALL

Working with drywall requires some special skills. Other than for the bulk weight, hanging drywall is fairly simple. But, finishing the drywall to get acceptable seams is quite another matter. There is an art to finishing drywall.

Drywall is far and away the leader in modern wall covering materials. It is inexpensive and produces an attractive wall or ceiling, when finished properly. A lot of do-it-yourselfers get in over their head with drywall, because they are not aware of what is involved in working with the heavy gypsum board. This section is going to show you how to hang and finish drywall in your project.

> **PRO POINTER**
> Drywall is heavy to hang and difficult to finish to a smooth surface. Few homeowners are capable of installing and finishing drywall with professional results.

MATERIAL CHOICES

The material choices for drywall are more numerous than you might think. There is fire-rated drywall for use in garages, where the garage shares a common wall or ceiling with habitable space. Moisture resistant drywall, which is usually green, is available for use in places with high humidity, like bathrooms.

Gypsum board is available in various thicknesses, they are: three-eighths of an inch, half-inch, and five-eighths of an inch. The overall size dimensions for wall board can be four feet by eight feet, four feet by 12 feet, and four feet by 16 feet. Professionals normally use four-by-twelve sheets to cut down on hanging time and seams. Four-by-eight sheets are much easier to handle and are the common choice of most homeowners.

Typical drywall construction consists of a finished side, normally white or cream colored, a gypsum center, and a paper backing. The edges of drywall may be straight, tapered, squared, beveled, rounded, or tongue-and-grooved.

TRADE TIP

Gypsum board is heavy. When carrying the heavy boards, it is best to carry them in a vertical position. If two people try to carry a board that is laid out in its full width, the weight of the board can cause it to break. Drywall is brittle and must be treated gently.

HANGING DRYWALL

When hanging drywall, the material can be attached to studs and joists with nails, screws, or staples. Most professional use drywall screws and electric screw guns to install the wallboard. One advantage to screws is that they are less likely to work loose than nails. If a nail works its way loose, it will dimple or pop the drywall finish.

When attaching drywall to joists and studs, nails should be driven extra deep, to create a dimple in the drywall. Screws should be run up tight, to make a depression in the wallboard. These depressions can be filled with joint compound to hide the nail and screw heads. When nailing, use a crown-head hammer. This type of hammer has a rounded-out head and makes good dimples.

Drywall can be cut in many ways. You can use a keyhole or drywall saw to cut your material. A jigsaw or saber saw will do a fine job of cutting gypsum. A utility knife is the tool used by most professionals when cutting drywall. This procedure requires you to score the drywall with the utility knife and then to break the drywall at the scored seam. Many people use T-squares, two-by-fours, or chalk lines to provide a straight cut.

HANGING CEILINGS

When both the walls and ceilings will be covered with drywall, it is best to start by hanging the ceilings. By hanging the ceilings first, the drywall installed on the stud walls will help to support the ceilings.

The drywall hung on a ceiling is attached to the exposed ceiling joists. Cut-outs will have to be made for any ceiling-mounted electrical boxes or fixtures. The hard part of this job is getting the drywall up on the ceiling. Due to its weight, drywall is not easy to install above your head. However, there is a way to reduce this burden.

By taking a couple of strips of scrap two-by-four material, you can make a brace to hold the drywall in place. Some people refer to this type of brace as a T-brace, and others call them a dead man. To make the brace, nail a length of two-by-four, about three feet long, onto the end of a two-by-four that is long enough to reach the ceiling, with a little left over.

Once this brace is made, it can be wedged under drywall to hold it to the ceiling. The T-arm will rest under the drywall and the long section of the brace will be wedged between the sub-floor and the ceiling. If two people raise the drywall to the ceiling, the dead-man can take the place of the second person, once it is wedged into place.

By using two tall ladders and two T-braces, it is possible to hang a ceiling by yourself. It is not easy, but it is possible. Sit the drywall on the top of the ladders. Leave a couple of feet of the wallboard hanging over each end of the ladders. Put the first T-brace under one end and raise the drywall with the brace. Wedge the brace against the floor and raise the other end of the drywall with the other brace. This will take some time and practice, but once you get the hang of it, you can install your ceilings without help.

HANGING WALLS

Hanging walls can be done by applying the drywall vertically or horizontally. You should choose the method that will result in the least waste and the fewest seams. If you hang your walls vertically, you will not need any help. Hanging the walls horizontally will generally result in fewer joints, but it is more difficult to do without a helper.

There are, however, some tricks that will make horizontal hanging easier in the absence of help.

You can nail large nails to the studs to provide temporary support for the drywall panel. Another way of doing this is to nail a two-by-four ledger horizontally across the wall. The drywall can rest on the ledger while you attach it to the studs. Of course, with either method you will have to make cut-outs for electrical boxes, water supplies, drain arms, and other items that should not be covered up.

CORNER BEAD

Metal corner bead is installed on the outside edges of most corners and exposed edges of drywall. These metal strips provide protection to exposed corners and edges. The strips are perforated and can be nailed or screwed to wall studs. The corner bead is designed to retain joint compound for a smooth finish.

APPLYING TAPE AND JOINT COMPOUND

When it comes to applying tape and joint compound, practice and patience will be required. This part of the job requires a special touch that must be developed through experience.

Some joint compound, or mud as it is called in the trade, needs to be mixed with water, but other types are ready to use right out of the bucket. Refer to the manufacturer's instructions on mixing your joint compound. You will use a wide putty knife, about four inches wide, to spread the mud.

The tape used in finishing drywall is not sticky. It is a wide band of paper that comes on a roll. The tape can be torn or cut, and it is flexible.

APPLYING THE FIRST COAT

When applying the first coat of mud, spread the joint compound over seams, corner bead, and dimples. Don't spread too much at a time. It is best to work one seam at a time. The first coat of mud should be about three inches wide, and it should be applied generously.

Once the mud is in place, lay a strip of tape on the mud and over the seam. Use the putty knife to work the tape down into the joint compound. The tape should sit deeply into the compound. Next, smooth out the mud and feather it away at the edges of the tape. Continue this process on all seams.

FIGURE 11-1
Expert drywall work.

When filling in nail dimples, tape is not necessary. Simply apply joint compound in the depressions until it is flush with the drywall. Smooth the compound out with your putty knife and let it dry.

You do not need tape when mudding in corner beads. The metal strips are meant to take the joint compound on directly. However, with inside corners, where there is no bead, tape is required. Run a line of joint compound down the inside corner in preparation for your tape. Cut the length of tape you will need and fold it to fit into the corner. Work the tape into the mud like you did with the other seams.

With all of this done, wait until the compound dries. Under average conditions, the mud should dry overnight. However, in damp or cold conditions, it may take longer for the mud to dry. When this is the case, a little heat will go a long way in speeding up the drying process. The heat should be distributed evenly and not in excess.

APPLYING THE SECOND COAT

After the first coat of joint compound is dry, you are ready to begin applying the second coat. The second coat is applied on top of the first coat, but it should be much wider. The first coat had a width of about three inches. The second coat should have a width of about six inches. Go over all of the original mud work with a second coating. This phase of the work will have to dry before you can move on.

THE THIRD COAT

The third coat is usually the final finish on the drywall. Before applying the last coat of mud, you have some sanding to do. Sand the compound first with a medium-grit sandpaper and then with a fine-grit sandpaper. A good dust mask is very helpful in this job. For sanding, you can use pieces of sandpaper, a sanding block, or a sanding block that attaches to a long handle. Use soft strokes in the sanding to avoid scarring the wallboard.

When you are ready to put on the third coat of mud, spread it with a width of about ten inches. As you spread the mud, feather the edges. The wider strip and feathered edges will make it easier to hide the seams. Cover the nail dimples with broad strokes and feather the edges. The final coat of mud is normally applied much lighter than the previous coats.

SANDING

After the final coat of mud has dried, you are ready for the finish sanding. Since the third coat of mud was applied in a thinner layer, it will be easier to sand. Use fine-grit sandpaper for the finish sanding. When this step is complete, you are ready to clean up and prepare to prime and paint the walls.

DID YOU KNOW?

An electric palm sander, when used with the right touch, will speed up the sanding process of preparing drywall compound for a final coat. However, electric sanders in inexperienced hands can damage drywall, so be careful and don't apply too much pressure or sand too long in the same spot at one time.

Gypsum Plaster – Metal Lath

Fire Rating	Design No.	Page
1-hr	OSU T-147	11
1-hr	OSU T-129	11
2-hr	UL U413	11
2-hr	NBS	11

Gypsum Plaster Fireproofing Columns (10WF49 or heavier)

Fire Rating	Design No.	Page
1-hr	BMS 92/40	12
2-hr	UL X402	12
3-hr	UL X402	12
4-hr	UL X402	12

Gypsum Plaster Fireproofing Beams (8WF24 or heavier)

Fire Rating	Design No.	Page
2-hr	UL R4197-1	12
3-hr	UL R4197-1	12

Veneer Plaster Partitions

Fire Rating	Design No.	Page
1-hr	U of Cal. E.S.6727	12
1-hr	U of Cal. E.S.6892	12

Gypsum Wallboard Partitions – Wood Framing

Fire Rating	Design No.	Page
45 min.	UL U317	12
1-hr	UL U305	12
1-hr	UL U309	13
1-hr	UL U340	13
1-hr	WHI 694-0200	13
1-hr	UL U312	13
2-hr	FM WP-360	13
2-hr	UL U301	13
1-hr	WHI 651-0319	14
2-hr	UL U302	13
2-hr	UL U371	14

Gypsum Wallboard Partitions – Steel Framing

Fire Rating	Design No.	Page
1-hr	OSU T-3296	14
1-hr	UL U420	14
1-hr	UL V401	14
1-hr	UL V438	14
1-hr	UL U451	14
1-hr	FM WP-45	15
1-hr	OSU T-1770	15
1-hr	UL U465	15
1-hr	UL V452	15
1-hr	FM WP-66	15
1-hr	FM WP-733	15

Fire Rating	Design No.	Page
1-hr	UL U410	16
1 1/2-hr	OSU T-3240	16
2-hr	UL V449	16
2-hr	UL V438	16
2-hr	UL U420	16
2-hr	UL U412	16
2-hr	UL U411	16
2-hr	WHI 495-0236	16
2-hr	UL V452	17
2-hr	ITS/WHI J98-32931	17
3-hr	UL U435	17
3-hr	WHI 694-0084	17
3-hr	UL V438	17
4-hr	UL U435	17
4-hr	WHI 694-108.1	17
4-hr	UL V438	17

Gypsum Wallboard Partitions – Steel Framing (load bearing)

Fire Rating	Design No.	Page
1-hr	UL U425	18
2-hr	FM WP-199	18
2-hr	UL U425	18
3-hr	UL U426	18

Gypsum Wallboard Partitions/Durasan Prefinished Gypsum Wallboard

Fire Rating	Design No.	Page
1-hr	FM WP-109	18
1-hr	UL U405	18
2-hr	UL U411	18

Gypsum Wallboard Partitions/Solid

Fire Rating	Design No.	Page
1-hr	FM WP-671	19
2-hr	UL U525	19
2-hr	FM WP-668	19
2-hr	UL U505	19
2-hr	UL U529	19

Gypsum Wallboard Partitions – Shaftwalls, Area Separation Walls

Fire Rating	Design No.	Page
1-hr	UL U499	19
1-hr	FM WP-755	19
2-hr	UL U498	19
2-hr	FM WP-545	19
2-hr	U of Cal. 75-19 ES 7407	19
2-hr	UL U429	19
2-hr	UL U497	19
2-hr	FM WP-636	19
2-hr	WHI 651-0500.05	19
2-hr	U of Cal. 75-17 ES 7408	19
2-hr	UL U428	20

FIGURE 11-2

Quick Selector Index—Fire/Sound. *(Courtesy of National Gypsum.)* *(continued on page 141)*

2-hr	FM WP-621	20
2-hr	FM WP-612	20
4-hr	UL V451	20
2-hr	WHI 694-0200.6	20
2-hr	WHI 651-0508	20
2-hr	UL U347	20

Gypsum Wallboard Column Fireproofing (light column)

Fire Rating	Design No.	Page
1-hr	UL X528	21
1 1/2-hr	UL X531	21
2-hr	UL X528	21

Gypsum Wallboard Column Fireproofing (heavy column)

Fire Rating	Design No.	Page
1-hr	UL X528	21
2-hr	UL X528	21
3-hr	UL X510	21
4-hr	UL X501	21
2-hr	UL X520	21
3-hr	UL X513	21

Gypsum Wallboard Beam Fireproofing

Fire Rating	Design No.	Page
2-hr	UL N501	22

Gypsum Wallboard Floor/Ceiling – Wood Framing (wood joist)

Fire Rating	Design No.	Page
1-hr	UL L522	22
1-hr	UL L501	22
1-hr	UL L515	22
1-hr	FM FC-181	22
1-hr	FM FC-193	22
1-hr	FM FC-172	22
2-hr	UL L505	22

Gypsum Wallboard Floor/Ceiling – Wood Framing (floor truss)

Fire Rating	Design No.	Page
1-hr	FM FC-442	23
1-hr	UL L528	23
1-hr	FM FC-448	23
1-hr	UL L558	23
1-hr	FM FC-214	23
2-hr	UL L538	23

Gypsum Wallboard Roof/Ceiling – Wood Framing (pitched roof truss)

Fire Rating	Design No.	Page
1-hr	UL P533	23

Gypsum Wallboard Floor/Ceiling – Light Gauge Steel Framing

Fire Rating	Design No.	Page
1-hr	UL L524	24
1 1/2-hr	UL L527	24
1-hr	UL L565	24

Gypsum Wallboard Floor/Ceiling – Steel Framing (steel joists with concrete floor)

Fire Rating	Design No.	Page
1-hr	OSU T-1936	24
1-hr	FM FC-134	25
2-hr	UL G503	24
2-hr	UL G514	25
3-hr	UL G512	25
2-hr	FM FC-134	25
2-hr	UL G523	25
2-hr	UL D502	25
2-hr	UL G222	25
2-hr	FM FC-299	25
1 1/2-hr	UL G259	25
1 1/2- hr	FM FC-300	25

Gypsum Wallboard Roof/Ceiling – Light Gauge Steel Framing (pitched roof truss)

Fire Rating	Design No.	Page
1-hr	UL P540	26
1-hr	UL P541	26
2-hr	UL P543	26

Gypsum Wallboard Roof/Ceiling – Steel Framing (steel joists)

Fire Rating	Design No.	Page
1-hr	FM RC-227	26

Gypsum Wallboard Horizontal Shaftwall Duct Protection

Fire Rating	Design No.	Page
2-hr	WHI 694-0300.1	26

FIGURE 11-2

Quick Selector Index—Fire/Sound. *(Courtesy of National Gypsum.) (continued)*

12

Interior Doors, Cabinets, and Trim

Once you reach the point of installing interior doors, cabinets, and trim, you are well on your way to a completed job. At this point, completion is not far away, but you are about to embark on what can be a tedious task.

When your job is finished, the insulation won't be seen. At the end of the job you will not notice the routing of the electrical wires or the plumbing. But, with doors, cabinets, and trim, you will see them on a daily basis. Since the finish work is what will be seen, it stands to reason that you will want this part of your work to be attractive. Rough work doesn't have to look good; it only has to be functional. Trim work must look good, or the entire job will suffer.

Trim work can be deceiving. It is not unusual for novices to watch a trim carpenter and assume they can do the same job. In reality, trim work can be demanding and frustrating. This phase of the job can also get expensive. Finish trim materials are not cheap. Unlike missing a cut on a two-by-four, a mistake in cutting a handrail can cost you plenty. While screwing cabinets to a wall may look simple, it can require extensive skill. This chapter is going to shed light on the often misunderstood phase of trim carpentry.

INTERIOR DOORS

When it comes to choosing interior doors, you have many options. The cost of these doors fluctuates greatly. Here are some key questions to ask yourself:

- Will you use flat luan doors or six-panel doors?

- If you decide on six-panel doors, will they be real wood or a composite material?

- Do you know the difference between a left-hand and a right-hand door?

- Should you buy standard slab doors or pre-hung units?

- What hardware should be used on the doors?

As you can see, the questions pertaining to interior doors can accumulate quickly. In this section, we are going to dissect these questions and answer them. Additionally, we are going to look at installation methods.

STANDARD DOORS

Standard doors are often called slab doors. These doors are sold individually and do not come with trim packages or pre-hung. The installation of a slab door is best left to professionals. There are many steps involved with installing a standard door. Beginners will be much better off when purchasing pre-hung door units. However, since some people will want to install standard doors, let's see how it is done.

DID YOU KNOW?
Standard doors are often called slab doors. These doors are sold individually and do not come with trim packages or pre-hung. The installation of a slab door is best left to professionals. There are many steps involved with installing a standard door.

BUILDING THE JAMB

Before standard doors can be hung, a door jamb must be built. A door jamb consists of a head jamb and two side jambs. Jamb material

FIGURE 12-1
When it comes to interior doors, there are many options from
which to choose—from basic to high-end quality and design.

> **PRO POINTER**
> When building a door jamb, you must take into consideration the size of the door and the height of the finish floor covering. Most standard doors have a height of 6 feet 8 inches. Door widths vary.

is normally a one-by material. The width of the jamb will be determined by the wall covering on the stud wall. If a standard half-inch drywall is used, the jamb will typically have a width of 4$\frac{9}{16}$ inch.

When building a door jamb, you must take into consideration the size of the door and the height of the finish floor covering. Most standard doors have a height of 6 feet and 8 inches. Door widths vary. On average, the jamb opening should be about 2½ inches wider than the door. Three inches is a standard figure for the gap above the door and between the jamb. Remember to allow for the finish floor covering. A floor covered with vinyl flooring will require the door to be hung lower than a floor covered with a pad and carpet.

Once the jamb is assembled, it should be set in place and leveled. It may be necessary to cut one of the side jambs to a shorter length to make the jamb level. The next step is to find the proper location for hinges.

INSTALLING HINGES

Normally, when installing door hinges, they are set with the bottom edge of the lower hinge about 11 inches above the bottom of the door. The upper hinge is usually mounted with its top edge about 7 inches below the top of the door. These measurements are not mandatory, but they are a good place to start. If a third hinge is used, it is commonly centered between the two primary hinges.

Lay the first hinge on the edge of the door. Allow the barrel of the hinge to protrude past the edge of the door by about $\frac{1}{8}$ inch. Trace around the hinge with a pencil or utility knife to mark the hinge location on the door. Next, place the door in the jamb. This is only a temporary setting to allow marking the hinge locations on the jamb. Once the door is in the jamb, allow a small clearance between the top of the door and the head jam, say about $\frac{1}{16}$ inch. Mark the jamb to indicate hinge locations.

At this point, you are ready to chisel recesses in the door and side jamb for the hinges. This is normally done with a sharp wood chisel. Start by cutting with the chisel running parallel with the door. Once cuts are made, chisel them out with the chisel perpendicular to the door. The recesses should be deep enough to allow the hinges to mount flush into them.

PRO POINTER

When installing hardware, you may have to drill the door. Some doors come pre-drilled for hardware and others don't. Before drilling your door, check the instructions that came with your door set.

SHIMMING THE HINGE JAMB

It is necessary to shim the door jamb to make it firm and level. The shim material can be scrap wood, but most carpenters used cedar shingles for shims. Start by shimming the side jamb where the hinges will be mounted. Place shims between the side jamb and the rough framing. Check the side jamb to see that it is level in both directions and nail through the side jamb and shims into the rough framing. Finish nails should be used for this application, normally eight-penny nails.

TRADE TIP

It is necessary to shim the door jamb to make it firm and level. The shim material can be scrap wood, but most carpenters use cedar shingles for shims.

HANGING THE DOOR

Before shimming the remainder of the jamb, you should hang the door. Start by removing the hinge pins from the hinges. Keep the hinge halves together, so they can be matched during the installation. Install the hinge plates on the door first. Be sure the mounting screws recess into the hinge plate. Next, install the hinge plates on the side jamb, matching the hinge-halves with the ones mounted on the door.

Hanging the door will be easier if you have someone to help, but it can be done alone. Lift the door into place and allow the hinge-halves to go together. When the top hinge-halves are in proper alignment, insert a hinge pin, but don't drive it tight. The pin should hold the hinge-halves together, but it should not be permanently set at this time. Continue this process, working from the top to the bottom.

SHIMMING THE REST OF THE JAMB

With the door in place, you are ready to shim the rest of the jamb. Place shims between the jamb and rough framing. When the jamb is level in all directions, try swinging the door through the jamb. Then, place the door in the closed position. When the door is closed, there should be approximately $1/16$ inch of open space between the edges of the door and the jamb. When the door is properly positioned, nail through the jamb and shims into the framing.

INSTALLING HARDWARE

When installing hardware, you may have to drill the door. Some doors come pre-drilled for hardware and others don't. Before drilling your door, check the instructions that came with your door set. Most door knobs require a hole just over 2 inches in diameter, but hardware requirements vary, so it is best to check and follow the instructions packed with your hardware. Most instructions will include a template to guide you in the cutting and drilling of your door. Once you have installed your latch, strike plate, and door knob, you are ready to put on the doorstop.

INSTALLING DOORSTOP TRIM

Installing doorstop trim is easy. Doorstop is sold in stock sizes. All you have to ask for is doorstop material. Close the door and make sure the latch is working. With the door closed, nail the doorstop into place. The doorstop will run vertically on each side jamb and horizontally along the head jamb. The stop should be nailed in place so that it is firm against the door, but not applying undue pressure. Use finish nails for this phase of your job, normally four-penny nails.

INSTALLING DOOR CASING

The last major step in your job is installing the door casing. Six-penny finish nails are frequently used for this part of the job. Cut your trim to fit around the door jamb. Hold the casing off of the edge of the jamb by about $1/8$ inch, to allow clearance for working with hinge pins. Once the trim is tacked into place and fits satisfactorily, drive the nails in tight. Use a nail punch to recess the nails into the trim. All that is left is to drive down the hinge pins, and you're done.

PRE-HUNG DOORS

Pre-hung doors will save you much time and frustration. When you buy pre-hung doors they come as a unit, ready to set into the rough opening. The door jamb is built, the door is hung and drilled for hardware, and the trim casing is even provided and pre-assembled. In my opinion, pre-hung doors are the only way to go, unless you just can't get the door you love in a pre-hung unit.

CABINETS

Hanging and setting cabinets can get tricky. When the floor or walls are out of level, creative adjustments must be made. While setting a base cabinet in place or screwing wall cabinets to the studs may look easy, it is not always so. Let's look at what you might encounter when working with cabinets.

BASE CABINETS

Base cabinets are cabinets that sit on the floor. When the floor and walls are level, base cabinets are easy to install, for the most part. Standard base cabinets are generally about $32\frac{1}{2}$ inches high. Once a countertop is installed on the base cabinets, the finished height is usually around 36 inches.

Cabinet materials might consist of solid wood, plywood, or particle board. Many production cabinets use a mixture of these materials.

PRO POINTER

Cabinet work requires special skills and is usually best left to professionals. An average homeowner can do the work if all the conditions are right, but this is rarely the case. Walls and floors can be out of square and out of plumb. This creates problems with cabinets. Unless you are an experienced carpenter, you should probably hire a skilled cabinet installer to install your cabinets.

Production cabinets are much more economical than custom cabinets, but even so, the cost of stock cabinets can blow your budget. Cabinets are often one of the largest single expenses in the finish stages of a job.

With base cabinets, there are many options. Do you want dovetail joints or butt joints? Dovetail joints will hold up better than butt joints. Base cabinets may have doors, drawers, appliance openings, or special accessories. Many base cabinets have a combination of drawers and doors. An important consideration in choosing a drawer base is how well the drawers

FIGURE 12-2
Cabinets are often one of the largest single expenses in the finish stages of a job, and prices vary greatly.

glide. If the drawers will see frequent use, and they usually do, insist on a cabinet with quality glides and rollers.

Before buying or installing your cabinets, you will need to design the layout. Will you need a sink base? Sink bases are wide base cabinets, usually with two doors, that are made to house a kitchen sink. Determining width requirements and corner cabinets is another part of your design. Most any store selling cabinets will be happy to come out and measure your job. Then, the supplier will often provide a sketch or computer drawing to show you what the proposed cabinets will look like. Make your design decisions and changes before buying the cabinets. Also take into consideration your need for filler strips and accessory pieces.

WALL CABINETS

Wall cabinets hang on walls. The height of standard wall cabinets will vary, but most are available with widths as narrow as 9 inches. When thinking of width, think in 3 inch increments, as this is how most wall cabinets are available. Do you want doors made to accommodate hardware pulls or finger grooves? This, of course, is a personal choice. When checking out wall cabinets, look for quality in the shelves and latches. Shelf holders should be adjustable, to allow various shelf heights. Magnetic latches are less likely to break and should last much longer that plastic latches.

INSTALLING CABINETS

Before installing your cabinets it is a good idea to check a few things. If cabinets are not installed level, drawers and doors may not operate properly. If the cabinets are too far out of level, they will be visually crooked. When dealing with new construction, the odds of leveling problems are less than when working with old walls and

DID YOU KNOW?

An important consideration in choosing a drawer base is how well the drawers glide. If the drawers will see frequent use, and they usually do, insist on a cabinet with quality glides and rollers.

TRADE TIP

Rather than hanging the cabinets one-by-one, you could join the cabinets on the floor and raise the entire row at one time. If you have enough help to lift the completed row, this method can be faster and easier.

floors. However, even in new construction, walls and floors are not always level. Before you begin installing your cabinets, confirm the floor and wall conditions. If these areas are out of plumb, you will need to shim your cabinets.

WALL CABINETS

Most people install wall cabinets first. This is done to avoid having previously installed base cabinets damaged during the installation of wall cabinets. The first consideration is how high to hang the cabinets.

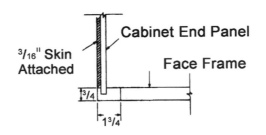

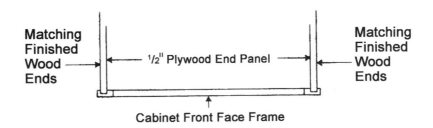

FIGURE 12-3
Cabinet components. (*Courtesy of Wellborn Cabinet, Inc.*)

This measurement varies, but a rule-of-thumb figure is about 84 inches above the floor. Once you determine the desired height, you should mark a level line as a reference point. Next, find the wall studs. If necessary, you can do this

by probing the wall where the cabinet will hang. The back of the cabinet will conceal any holes from the probing. Make a measurement from the corner to the stud for reference. Most wall studs will be installed 16 inches on center.

When you begin your installation, start with a corner cabinet. Hanging wall cabinets is much easier if you have some help. Getting cabinets into position and keeping them in place is difficult for one person. Even with help, you will probably want to use some prop sticks to hold the wall cabinets up. These prop sticks can be two-by-fours.

Once the cabinet is in place and level, drill holes through the back of the cabinet and into the wall studs. The holes should be kept near the top of the cabinet. There is frequently a mounting strip in the cabinet for the screws to penetrate. Install screws to hold the cabinet in place. At this time, the screws don't need to be tight. In most cases there will be some shimming and final adjustments to be made before the screws are run all the way in.

After the first cabinet is installed, install the adjacent cabinet in the same manner. When you have two wall cabinets in place, it is time to attach them. The first step in joining the two cabinets is getting them into proper alignment. Adjust the cabinets until they are in the proper horizontal and vertical position. You can use C-clamps to hold the cabinets together and in place. Double check your alignment. Then, use ¼ inch screws to attach the two cabinets to each other. Some people prefer nuts and bolts for the joining process. The screws or bolts should be placed near the top and bottom of the cabinet side-walls.

Once the row of cabinets is complete and in position, you can screw the units to the wall tightly. Frequently check to be sure the cabinets are remaining level. Once the row is installed, you can add filler strips as needed. The filler strips will be of the same finish as the cabinets and will conceal any gaps where the cabinets meet walls or other objects.

Depending upon your choice in designs, you may choose to install a soffit or valance. These are trim boards, in the same finish as the cabinets, to close up the area between the top of the cabinets and the ceiling. To install these items, you must first attach a nailing surface to the ceiling. The nailing surface is attached to the ceiling to provide a place for the trim to be attached.

BASE CABINETS

Base cabinets are a little easier to install. You should start with a corner cabinet and build out your row. It may be necessary to shim under the cabinets to keep them level. Base cabinets should be attached to each other in the same way as wall cabinets. When checking to see that the base cabinets are level, check both vertically and horizontally.

If you are working with a base cabinet that doesn't have a back, you will need to install cleats. Cleats are just strips of wood that support the countertop. The cleats, or ledgers, as they are sometimes called are attached to wall studs. The ledgers should be installed level and at the same height as the front of the cabinet.

PRO POINTER
Base cabinets are a little easier to install. You should start with a corner cabinet and build out your row. It may be necessary to shim under the cabinets to keep them level.

COUNTERTOPS

Countertops are the next process in finishing your cabinet installation. There are numerous choices in countertop styles and materials. Your supplier should be able to show you samples of what is available. The easiest way to work with countertops is to have them measured and provided by professionals. If you give your dealer the brand and model of your sink, he can cut the sink hole for you. Then, when the countertop is delivered, all you have to do is install it. It is customary to wait until the cabinets are installed to order the top. Since jobs don't always go as they are drawn on paper, ordering the top before the cabinets are installed could result in a top that will not fit.

When you look down on your base cabinets, you should see some triangular blocks of wood in the corners. These triangles provide a place to attach the counter to the cabinet. Before sitting the counter in place, drill holes through these mounting blocks. Keep the holes in a location that will allow you to install screws from inside the cabinet. It may be a good idea to drill the holes on an angle, toward the center of the cabinet, to allow more freedom in installing screws.

Sit the countertop in place and check its fit. When the top is in position, install screws from below, through the holes in the triangular blocks. Make sure the screws are not long enough to penetrate the counter and ruin the top.

If you must cut your own sink hole, use the template that came with your sink, if you are using a new sink. If you are using an old sink, turn the sink upside down and sit it on the counter, in the proper location. Lightly trace around the sink rim with a pencil. Remove the sink and draw a new outline inside the original tracing. When guessing at how large the hole should be it is best to cut it too small, rather than too large. You must make the hole smaller than the lines you traced around the sink. There must be enough counter left to support the rim of the sink.

To cut the sink hole, drill a hole in the countertop. Using a reciprocating saw, like a jig saw, place the blade in the hole you drilled. Cut slowly along your interior line. Don't get your lines confused, cutting to the outside line will mean owning a ruined countertop. When you have your hole, try putting the sink in it. If necessary, expand the opening until the sink will fit.

If you are working with limited space, there are many types of specialty cabinets available. Pantry cabinets can provide a lot of storage in a little space. Some cabinets are equipped with built-in units, like tables and pull-down bins. When installing cabinets in small bathrooms, proper cabinet selection can provide additional storage.

INTERIOR TRIM

Interior trim is easy to install, if you are good at cutting angles. First, find and mark stud locations. You will use six-penny finish nails with most trim applications. A backsaw and miter box is an inexpensive way to cut angles on trim material. Most professionals use power miter saws, but a miter box and backsaw will work fine.

The two most common baseboards are clam and colonial. Colonial is considered to be the standard in quality construction. Baseboard is installed along walls to conceal gaps between the wallboard and floor. When carpeting the floor, some people install the baseboard low and allow the carpet to conceal part of it. Other tradespeople hold the baseboard up to allow for the thickness of the carpet and pad.

Cutting corners is not difficult with a miter box. An electric miter saw is even better. However, getting used to fitting the angles together can take a little time. If you are dealing with a long run of baseboard you may have to make a joint in the run. Instead of butting the two pieces of trim together, you should cut angles that will allow the two trim pieces to lay over each other. This is often called a lap joint. By cutting a lap joint, you have a more even flow in your trim. When baseboard meets door casing, it simply butts against the casing. If baseboard heating units will be attached to the walls, omit baseboard trim in the area to be occupied by the heating unit.

If the finish floor covering will be a thin vinyl material, shoe mold should be used. In this pro-

DID YOU KNOW?
Interior trim is easy to install, if you are good at cutting angles.

TRADE TIP
Cutting corners is not difficult with a miter box. An electric miter saw is even better.

cedure, install the baseboard trim first. Then, install the finish floor. After the floor is in place, add shoe mold. The shoe mold is a small trim piece that covers the joints where the flooring meets the baseboard.

Chair rail and crown molding are installed with the same basic techniques. Chair rail goes on the wall, at a height to prevent the backs of chairs from damaging the wall. Crown molding is installed at the top of the wall, where the wall meets the ceiling. There are other types of trim, but once you are comfortable with cutting angles, you will be able to work with any of the trim materials.

FINAL COMMENTS

As a final comment, remember to take your time in doing your finish work. You must be willing to be patient and precise if you want a good looking job. Trim work is not hard physically, but it is mentally demanding.

13

Priming , Painting, and Staining

Anyone can do paint and stain work, right? Well, almost anyone can do it, but it takes special knowledge to do it right. The public generally perceives painting as a job that doesn't require in-depth knowledge or skill. This is a false perception. Just because painters don't go through the same professional licensing requirements as plumbers and electricians do, it doesn't mean they don't have to know what they are doing.

I will admit that painting is one phase of a job that most homeowners can do on their own and achieve satisfactory results. However, how you go about your painting can have much to do with how long the job holds up and how well the job looks. This chapter is not going to turn you into a professional painter; you would need years of field experience and instruction to become a truly competent professional. What this chapter is going to do is show you the easy way to paint or stain your project and the pitfalls to avoid.

PRO POINTER

Due to the danger of working at heights with exterior painting, such as in the case of painting a dormer, you may be well advised to contract this work out to professional painters. It will do you little good to try saving money by being your own painter only to wind up hurt and missing work due to a fall.

EXTERIOR PAINTING

Exterior painting could include painting siding, windows, exterior trim, foundations, or railings. If you are building a dormer, you will have some high-elevation exterior painting to do. This work, primarily due to its location, can get dangerous. Before painting your dormer, exercise good judgment and care in safety procedures.

Some dormers can be painted while standing on the surrounding roof, but most will require the use of ladders or scaffolding. With whatever method you use to reach the area to be painted, make sure the climbing device is secure and safe. It is a wise idea to cordon off the area around your ladder to avoid having someone run into it, knocking you off. Also, be extremely careful when handling ladders and the like around electrical wires.

TYPES OF PAINTS AND PRIMERS

The two types of paints to consider are latex and oil-based paint. Most painters believe if a house is to be painted white, it should have an oil-based primer and paint. It is generally thought best to use an oil-based primer and a latex paint if the house will be painted a color other than white.

Primer is normally white. If you are painting your house white, don't worry about having the primer tinted. However, if you are painting with a color other than white, ask your paint dealer to tint the primer to match your finish color. Avoid tinting the primer to much darker or much lighter than the finish paint.

Should you use a flat paint or a gloss paint? Flat paint is normally used for siding, with gloss paint being applied to trim and windows. Gloss paint is easier to clean, but it shows more irregularities in the painted surface.

PREPARING TO PAINT

When preparing to paint, you should consider the use of drop cloths. You should protect the surrounding roof, existing home, and lawn and shrubbery with drop cloths. Paper drop cloths are available, easy to use, inexpensive, and a good choice for the occasional painter. Plastic drop cloths are slippery and do not contain paint well. Light canvas drop cloths are the professional choice, but these are expensive and are not needed for most homeowner jobs.

> **TRADE TIP**
> Many people don't think about using drop cloths when they are doing exterior painting. The same people who would never consider painting their living rooms without a drop cloth are likely to forget this step of protection when working outside. Cover areas that you don't want stray paint to cover.

Your paint dealer will shake your paint for you, but you should mix it again before using it. Too many people try to use the little wooden stirrers to mix paint in a gallon can. This procedure is not effective in obtaining a good mix. Pour the contents of the gallon cans into a larger container, like a five-gallon bucket. The larger container will allow you to mix the paint more thoroughly.

METHODS OF APPLICATION

> **DID YOU KNOW?**
> Rollers don't work well with most types of siding and sprayers can get messy, especially if the wind is blowing.

The standard methods of application for paint include brushing, rolling, and spraying. For dormer additions, a 4 inch brush is probably the best choice. You should also have a 1½ inch or 2 inch brush for painting windows and small trim. A 3 inch brush is good for window frames and some trim. Foam applicators are also good for painting trim. Normally, nylon brushes are used with latex paint and bristle brushes are used with oil-based paints. Rollers don't work well with most types of siding and sprayers can get messy, especially if the wind is blowing.

Start painting at the top of the exterior wall and work your way down. If you will be painting window grids or trim a different color or with a different paint, paint the windows first. If you don't, when you come back to paint the windows, you may damage the paint on the siding. Apply enough primer paint to cover the surface, but don't lay it on too heavy. What you want is a good coat of primer, followed by an even coat of finish paint. It is not a good idea to paint a surface that is bathed in direct sunlight.

Check with the manufacturer's suggestions, but most paint should not be applied in the temperature is below 50° F. or if it is extremely hot.

If you must thin your paint, do it a little at a time and in a container other than the mix bucket. Most painters use a small pail to hold the paint they are using at the time. This pail is a good place to thin the paint. If you miscalculate the thinning, you have wasted only a small percentage of your paint, not the entire mix bucket.

Apply the paint with the grain of the wood, normally horizontally. If you use an oil-based material, the painting surface must be completely dry. If it has rained recently, postpone your painting until the sun has dried the siding.

EXTERIOR STAINING

Exterior staining is not the same as painting. Stain is available in latex or oil, but oil-based stain is the common choice among professionals. Latex stain does not penetrate the wood as well as oil stain. When choosing a type of stain, you will normally have three choices: solid, semi-solid, and semi-transparent.

SOLID STAIN

Solid stains may be described as looking like a thin paint. Unlike most stains, solid stains can be applied over paint. This procedure is usually only practiced in special circumstances, but it is possible.

> **DID YOU KNOW?**
> As you go about your staining you should stir the stain in the container frequently. The pigment in stain will settle and cause the job to render different color shades if it is not stirred regularly. Don't hesitate to use a lot of stain, the more the better. Unlike paint, stain should be applied liberally.

SEMI-SOLID STAIN

Semi-solid stains provide excellent penetration and protection of wood. While the name, semi-solid, may imply a thick, paint-like substance, semi-solid stain is thin and does not provide a heavy visual cover.

SEMI-TRANSPARENT STAIN

Semi-transparent stains are at their best on rough wood surfaces. These stains protect against moisture damage and are available in a wide range of colors.

> **PRO POINTER**
> When choosing a stain, it is best to try a little on a sample of the wood you will be applying it on. Due to the nature of stain, it will take on different looks on various types of wood.

APPLICATION METHODS

Stains are usually best applied with a brush; however, they can be applied with a sprayer or a roller. You can even apply stain with a rag, sponge, or special

> **TRADE TIP**
> Latex stain does not penetrate wood. When using latex, apply two coats, but don't go back wiping off excess stain.

staining mittens. If you choose to use a brush, buy one with natural bristles. Synthetic brushes do not work as well as natural bristle brushes. It is advisable to apply two coats of stain, and unlike painting, the second coat should be applied while the first coat is still wet. After your second coat has been drying for an hour or so, go over it with a sponge or rag to remove stain that did not penetrate the wood.

INTERIOR PAINTING OF WALLS AND CEILINGS

Interior painting of new walls is a little less stressful than being perched high upon an extension ladder outside. For this type of painting, a good stepladder should get you to all the surfaces you need to paint.

> **TRADE TIP**
> The first step in preparing a new room for paint is cleaning. You should vacuum the room to remove all dust. If you don't, your paint will become textured with dust clumps.

PREPARATION

The first step in preparing a new room for paint is cleaning. You should vacuum the room to remove all dust. If you don't, your paint will become textured with dust clumps. You should be working over a sub-floor, so drop cloths are not necessary.

APPLYING INTERIOR PAINT

When applying interior paint, many contractors use only one coat of primer and one coat of paint. If the walls are in good shape, this is all that should be needed, but some professionals prefer to apply two coats of primer for a better looking job.

Normal procedure is to start with the ceiling. It has become common for drywall finishers to texture ceilings. When this is done, paint is often mixed in with the joint compound. If you choose to go this route, there will be no need for further painting of the ceiling. If you are performing a traditional paint job on the ceiling, a roller will be used. Sprayers are frequently used by professionals and are becoming increasingly popular with homeowners. When using a sprayer it will take a little practice to get the hang of setting the spray and giving even distribution of the paint.

When you paint ceilings with a roller, you will have to cut in along the joint between walls and ceilings with a brush. Using a two or three-inch brush, apply a strip of paint to the ceiling. The strip should only be a few feet long. As soon as you have this strip of wet

PRO POINTER

The decision between latex and oil paint is up to you. Most people use a latex primer and paint. When buying your primer, have it tinted to match the finish color.

paint, lay down the brush and pick up the roller. An extension handle in the roller will save you from making so many trips up and down a

FIGURE 13-1
Professional painting equipment in use. *(Courtesy of National Gypsum.)*

ladder. Use the roller to roll paint on the ceiling and over the wet strip. It is important to do your cut-ins a little at a time. If you try to cut in the whole ceiling before rolling on the paint, the cut-in section will dry. When you roll fresh paint over the dried cut-in, you will get two different looks.

Continue this brush-roller combination until the ceiling is complete. Don't be stingy with your paint. When you roll paint out too thin, it will dry without covering the surface. When the ceiling is done, you can start on the walls. Again, you will have to cut-in the joint between wall and ceiling, this time applying your paint to the wall. Work in small sections and keep the brush-and-roller relay going, so that the paint doesn't dry out.

After the first coat of paint, you may see imperfections that had been invisible. You may need to take time between the first and second coat to touch up the drywall. If you do perform touch-up work, be sure to vacuum any dust created before you return to painting.

Textured ceilings are very popular. If you choose to texture your ceiling, there will be many options available to you. Some contractors use drywall mud to create a ceiling texture, and others use special mixes designed just for texturing. You can use a variety of devices to apply texture. Some of your options are: a stiff paint brush, a stipple paint roller, a stiff round brush, or a trowel.

PAINTING INTERIOR TRIM

The painting of interior trim can be done before, during, or after painting the walls and ceilings. Many professionals recommend painting the trim in the same stages as you paint the walls. Normally, trim work is painted with a gloss paint and walls are painted with a flat paint. However, it is not unusual to have walls painted with gloss paint in kitchens or bathrooms. The gloss paint is easier to clean. Since you are likely to use two different types of paint and probably two different colors, you will have to switch back and forth between walls and trim if you paint both in the same phases.

> **TRADE TIP**
> Filling the holes from recessed finish nails will be required before final painting is done. You can use wood putty and a small putty knife to fill and smooth out these holes.

Why would you go to the trouble of switching back and forth at the same phases? If you paint the walls to completion it is likely you will accidentally get some trim paint on the walls. By alternating between trim and walls in the same phase, you reduce the risk of creating extra work for yourself. However, many people will choose to paint the walls and then paint the trim when the walls are finished. This is fine if you are careful not to get trim paint on the walls.

SURPRISES

Surprises often occur with painting. One such surprise is the affect the primer coat will have on some wood trim. Even if your trim is smooth when you apply the first coat of primer, the wood may become rough after the paint dries. This roughness can be annoying to anyone dusting and cleaning the trim. The roughness may be enough to snag cleaning rags and cause aggravation. After applying the first coat, check the texture of the trim. You may want to go over it with a light-grit sandpaper or steel wool to remove the rough spots. Vacuum the dust residue from the sanding before proceeding with your painting.

CUTTING-IN WINDOWS AND TRIM

The cutting-in of windows and trim should be done as described

> **DID YOU KNOW?**
> Some people don't use sealers on stained trim and others do. If you want to seal the trim, you can use a varnish or polyurethane. It is recommended to sand the trim between coats and to apply two coats of sealer.

in the earlier section on walls and ceilings. Work small areas and work with wet paint. When cutting-in or edging, you can use a piece of cardboard to protect surfaces you don't want painted.

STAINING TRIM

The staining of trim is often done before the trim is installed. One word of caution, if you plan to stain your trim, be sure to get clear wood, also known as stain-grade trim. This trim is a little more expensive than finger-joint trim, but it is the only type of trim to use when staining. Finger-joint trim can be painted without problems, but if you stain it, all the little finger-joints will show through the stain. If you are ordering pre-hung doors, specify stain-grade or clear trim. I have seen houses with stain-grade trim on the baseboards and finger-joint trim around the doors. This makes an odd and unappealing combination when the trim is stained.

A staining mitt or brush will make fast work of staining trim. If you are using an oil-based stain and a brush, use a bristle brush. Trim should be stained before the walls are painted. It is commonly stained before it is installed. Stain the trim and install it after it has dried. Go back and fill the nail holes with colored putty. This type of putty is available in paint stores. Then, touch-up the nail holes and cut marks with new stain. This is the fastest and easiest way to stain the trim.

FINAL WORDS

There you have it. You now know the basics for painting and staining your new project. Your paint dealer can provide more detailed information on the products you choose to use.

14

Floor Coverings

Floor coverings can take many forms. You can choose from carpet, vinyl sheet goods, ceramic tile, hardwood, softwood, and other options. Within each category are sub-categories. The decisions required for choosing a finish floor covering and accessories can be complicated.

Installing finish floors requires special tools and skills. The tools can be rented or purchased, but the skills must be learned. With the cost of flooring, mistakes get expensive fast. This is another area of your job where it might pay to call in professionals.

This chapter is going to introduce you to many types of flooring and the tools and principles needed to install them. You will learn the importance of carpet padding and the role it plays in the life of a carpet. There will be advice on when and where to use the various types of flooring. By the time you complete the chapter, you will have a good working knowledge of floor coverings and whether you want to do the job yourself or find a competent contractor. You will have enough knowledge to make sound decisions in choosing your materials.

Carpet has become the standard floor covering for most rooms. Wall-to-wall carpeting dominates nearly every room in the home, except for bathrooms and kitchens. Since carpet is the leader in floor coverings, we will start our tour with carpeting.

TYPES OF CARPETING

There are numerous types and grades of carpeting. Much of the decision on what type of carpet to buy will depend on the location of its intended installation. Let's look at some of the various types of carpet and where they are most likely to be used in your home.

LOOP-PILE AND CUT-PILE CARPET

Loop-pile and cut-pile carpet are the type found in most homes. Loop-pile carpet consists of fibers that are stitched into a backing. If the fibers are not cut, the carpet is loop-pile. If the fibers are cut, it is a cut-pile carpet. Carpet materials include acrylic, nylon, and polyester. Acrylic material enjoys a long life. Nylon carpet is very strong and resistive to staining. Polyester products are generally colorful and shiny.

Loop-pile carpet is usually installed over a pad and can be used in any room of the house. The quality of the carpet pad plays a vital role in the life of the carpet. If money is an issue, buy an excellent pad and a good carpet. Not only will the high-grade pad be comfortable to walk on, it will extend the life of the carpet.

Loop-pile carpet is normally laid over a pad and stretched to attach to tackless strips. The strips are either nailed or glued to the sub-floor. When the carpet is stretched onto the strips, angled teeth on the strip grab and hold the carpet.

TRADE TIP

Let me give you an experiment that you can try at your local carpet supplier. Take a carpet sample and lay it on a top-of-the-line pad. Stand on the carpet, and when you step off, see how long it takes for your footprints to disappear. Next, move the carpet sample to a low-grade pad, and try the same test. You will see that the same carpet on the good pad recovers its shape much more quickly than it does when on the inexpensive pad.

FOAM-BACK CARPET

Foam-back carpet is often considered a commercial carpet, but it is also a good choice for basement installations. Foam-back carpet is normally laid on the floor directly, without additional padding. The foam backing is glued or taped to the floor. If you are cost conscious and finishing a basement, foam-back carpet is well worth investigating.

CARPET SQUARES

Carpet squares offer another possibility. These squares of carpet have an adhesive backing and are simply pressed into place on the sub-floor. The tiles are easy to install.

PLANNING A CARPET INSTALLATION

Planning a carpet installation requires some thought. Carpet has a pile and the pile all leans in one direction. Carpet looks its best when you are facing the pile. For this reason, it is customary to install carpet with the pile pointing toward the entrance of a room.

Most carpet is made in widths that do not exceed 12 feet. If your room has a dimension greater than 12 feet, you will probably have to seam your carpet. However, with enough searching, you may find a brand offering wider widths. If you have to seam your carpet, keep the seam out of high-traffic areas.

INSTALLING LOOP-PILE AND CUT-PILE CARPETING

Installing loop-pile and cut-pile carpeting can be tricky. The first order of business is installing the tackless strips. In the trade, some professionals refer to these strips as tack strips. In any event, the strips are normally about four feet long and have sharp, angled teeth, to bite into the carpet. Tack strips come in different sizes, check with your carpet supplier for the proper size to use with your carpet and pad.

The tackless strips should be installed around the perimeter of the area to be carpeted. For doorways and cased openings, you will want to install metal trim strips. These strips are either folded over or nailed on top of the carpet to give a finished edge that people will not trip over.

Tackless strips should be installed with a uniform distance from the wall. Check with your carpet supplier for the proper distance to maintain between the edge of the strip and the wall. A rule-of-thumb distance is a gap equal to two-thirds the thickness of the carpet.

PUTTING IN THE PAD

When putting in the pad, the tackless strips form a boundary. The pad should be installed to cover all the floor area within the strips, but the pad should not extend onto the strips. Check the manufacturer's recommendations to determine which side of the pad should lie of the floor.

Padding does not have to be installed in one piece. It is permissible to install padding in sections. When padding is being installed on a wood sub-floor, it is usually stapled to the floor. If installing on a concrete floor, use an approved adhesive to hold the pad in place.

> **DID YOU KNOW?**
> Padding does not have to be installed in one piece. It is permissible to install padding in sections.

CUTTING THE CARPET

The cutting of the carpet should not be done until the carpet is unrolled, flattened out, and at room temperature. Cut the carpet so that there will be at least three inches of extra carpet in all directions. If you are working with a cut-pile carpet, you will cut it from the back. Make your measurements and use a chalk line or straightedge to make an even cut along the carpet backing. The cut can be made with a utility knife.

Loop-pile carpet should be cut from the finished side, rather than on the backing. Make your measurement and use a straightedge to keep the cut straight. The cutting can be done with a utility knife. There are also special carpet-cutting tools that can be used for this part of the job. One such tool is a row-running knife.

LAYING THE CARPET

Laying the carpet will require the use of a tool that stretches the carpet. You might use a knee-kicker or a power stretcher. Either of these tools can be rented at most tool centers.

Put the carpet in place. You should have excess carpet turned up on all walls. Use a utility knife to cut the carpet at corners. Start the cut at the top of the upturned carpet and extend to a point close to the tack strip.

If your carpet must be seamed, the seam should be made before stretching the carpet. At the point of the seam, the two pieces of carpet should overlap each other by about one inch. Make sure the pile of both pieces of carpet is running in the same direction. Using

FIGURE 14-1
Carpeting can add to the warmth of a room and is especially popular in bedrooms.

TRADE TIP

Installing carpet is not simple, and I advise you to give serious consideration to hiring a professional for this part of your job.

a row-running knife, cut a straight line along the edge of the overlapped carpet. The knife will run along the edge of the top piece of carpet, cutting the bottom piece of carpet.

When the cut is complete, remove the cut strip from beneath the top piece of carpet. Lay the edges of both pieces of carpet back to expose the floor. Now you will lay a strip of hot-melt seaming tape on the floor. The tape should be laid so that the center of the tape is in line with the center point of where the two pieces of carpet will meet.

Running a hot iron over the seaming tape will activate it. Heat only small sections at a time and maintain an iron temperature of about 250°F. As the tape becomes sticky, roll the edges of the carpet pieces into place and butt them together. Continue this process, in small sections, until the complete seam is made.

Now you are ready to stretch the carpet. Ideally, you should have both a knee-kicker and a power stretcher. When you rent these tools, ask the supplier to instruct you in the proper use of the tools. Start the stretching in a corner. Using the knee-kicker, attach the carpet to the tackless strips on two walls at a corner.

Once the first corner is secured, use the power stretcher to secure the corner directly opposite of the corner already done. Power stretchers have the ability to telescope out to long lengths, in order to cover whole rooms. The knee-kicker will be used to secure the carpet between the previously secured locations. Basically, two walls are done with the knee-kicker and two walls are done with the power stretcher.

When all of the carpet is attached to the tackless strips, you can cut away the excess carpet with a utility knife. Run the knife along the top of the installed carpet, cutting off the excess that is rolled up on the wall. Then, use a flat bit screwdriver to tuck the remaining excess carpet into the gap between the tack strip and the wall.

For the carpet at doorways and openings, cut it to size and bend down the metal strip on top of the carpet. Use a wide block of wood and hammer to drive the metal strip down tight. Place the block of wood on the strip and tap the block with the hammer. Do not hit the strip with just a hammer, the strip will be damaged. If you are using a nail-on strip of metal, put the metal in place and tack it down.

INSTALLING FOAM-BACK CARPET

Installing foam-back carpet is much different than installing cut-pile or loop-pile carpet. There are no tackless strips needed, and it is not necessary to install separate padding. Foam-back carpet has a thin, built-in pad as a part of the carpet. You will not need stretchers, but you will need some adhesive or carpet tape.

You should buy an adhesive that is recommended for the carpet you are installing. Your carpet dealer can advise you on what your specific needs will be. If you prefer to use tape to secure your carpet, the carpet dealer can recommend and supply the two-sided tape.

Cut your foam-back carpet to a size to fit the area to be covered. It is a wise idea to make the initial cut a little larger than you think is needed. Lay the carpet in place and check the fit. Remove the carpet and trowel adhesive on the floor or install strips of carpet tape. Your carpet dealer can tell you at what intervals and in what amounts to use your adhesive or tape.

Place the carpeting over the tape or adhesive and work out any wrinkles in the carpet. You can use a length of two-by-four to push the wrinkles out. By lying the board on the carpet, with the wide side down, push the board to the edge of the carpet, removing the wrinkles. When the carpet is flat, trim off the excess. If necessary, install shoe molding to hide the joint between the carpet and wall.

VINYL FLOORING

Sheet vinyl flooring is a common choice for bathrooms and kitchens, and sometimes, basements. Sheet vinyl is generally more durable and easier to clean than individual vinyl tiles. Most vinyl sheet goods are available in widths of six or 12 feet.

> **PRO POINTER**
> The surface conditions of the area to be covered with vinyl are important. The surface should be flat and without cracks, bumps, or holes. Vinyl can be installed on wood or concrete, but if the surface is not flat, imperfections will show up in the finish flooring.

Vinyl flooring, like carpet, can be a challenge to install. If you are willing to take your time and work precisely, you should be able to do the job yourself.

SURFACE CONDITIONS

The surface conditions of the area to be covered with vinyl are important. The surface should be flat and without cracks, bumps, or holes. Vinyl can be installed on wood or concrete, but if the surface is not flat, imperfections will show up in the finish flooring.

Cracks in concrete floors, or even wood floors, can be filled with special compounds, designed for the purpose. Thin underlay can be applied to even out the floor and cover bad spots. The key is to have a surface that is flat, clean, dry, and free of oil, grease, or wax.

PREP THE VINYL

Before installation, prep the vinyl. Roll the flooring up with the finish side facing outward. Leave the vinyl rolled up for about a day. When possible, maintain an even temperature of about 65°F. for the prep period and installation.

SEAMS

Seams for vinyl are done differently than those with carpet. If the flooring will need a seam, make the seam before installing the flooring. Lay the two pieces of flooring in place so that they overlap. Make sure the pattern of the floor meets and matches. Using a straightedge and a utility knife, cut through both pieces of flooring where the seam will be made. Remove the scrap flooring and attach the two pieces to the floor at the seam. Use a hand roller to press the flooring down on the adhesive or tape. Then, cover the seam with a sealing compound.

LAYING VINYL FLOORING

When laying vinyl flooring, the vinyl should be laid out in the room with enough excess vinyl that the flooring rolls up on the walls. Use a utility knife to cut the vinyl where it must be fitted around corners. The vinyl may be held in place by adhesive, tape, staples, or a combination of them all.

Once the vinyl is in position, use a floor roller to roll out wrinkles. You can rent the necessary hand and floor rollers at tool rental centers. When the vinyl is flat, you must cut away the excess flooring. The utility knife can be run along a straightedge to cut the vinyl where it meets the walls. Baseboard or shoe molding will then be installed to hide the joint between floor and wall.

DID YOU KNOW?

When shopping for flooring, try to see a large section of the flooring on display. Choosing from small samples can be disappointing. A finished floor can look much different than a small sample did in a showroom. If you prefer to work with individual squares of vinyl, instead of sheet goods, there is a good selection of quality vinyl tiles available. You can use vinyl tiles to create your own designs. Sheet vinyl can be purchased with designs imprinted into the vinyl. If you prefer a uniform style, without designs, there are a host of choices from which to choose.

CERAMIC TILE

Ceramic tile is often found in the bathrooms and kitchens of high-quality homes. When it comes to tile, there are many different types and styles from which to choose. There are also a number of ways to install the various tile floorings. Because of the countless options in tile and the limited space in this chapter, I will concentrate on the most common methods of installing a tile floor.

MATERIALS

Materials for a tile floor can consist of quarry tile, mosaic tile, and glazed ceramic tile. Quarry tile is big and comes in natural clay colors. Mosaic tile is small and generally comes with numerous tiles connected to a backing or sheet of paper. The mosaic tile is placed on the paper or backing in a pattern, and each pattern usually covers about one square foot. Glazed ceramic tile may have a shiny finish or a matte finish. Ceramic tile may be bought as squares or rectangles. Sizes for ceramic tile vary from about four-inch squares up to about six-inch squares. Rectangular tile is often in a dimension of approximately four inches by six inches. Tile is available in a multitude of shapes.

SUB-FLOOR CONDITIONS

Sub-floor conditions are important for tile. Tile can be laid on concrete or wood. When applying tile to wood sub-floors, the sub-floor should be covered with an underlay. The underlay should be at least

FIGURE 14-2
Tile flooring is a great choice for bathrooms and kitchens.

⅜ of an inch thick and should be installed with ⅛ of an inch expansion gaps between the sheets. If a concrete floor is in bad shape, fill cracks and level the floor with a mortar mix. Allow the mortar to cure before laying tile.

> **DID YOU KNOW?**
> Ceramic tile can give your new space many different looks. You can buy tiles with designs on them. You might opt for a black and white checker-board look, or you might prefer diamond accents.

BEDDING THE TILE

Bedding the tile can be done in several ways. The most common way is to set the tile into an adhesive. For a wood sub-floor, the adhesive may be organic or epoxy. If the surface area where the tile will be installed is damp, use an epoxy adhesive. When laying tile on concrete, use a bond coat of mortar or adhesive. An older method for bedding tile is the deep-set method. This requires a bed of mortar, about one inch thick, to be put on the sub-floor. Then,

> **PRO POINTER**
> Large tile jobs and tile work that has complicated patterns should be left to professionals. It takes considerable skill to make a picture-perfect tile job come to be.

another bed of mortar is applied to the first, to hold the tile. The deep-set method adds considerable weight to the floor and has basically been replaced with thin-set adhesives. The choice for adhesives is often determined by the manufacturer's recommendations and the location and use of the tile. Check with your tile dealer for specifics.

GROUT

Grout is the material placed between tiles to prevent water and dirt from collecting between the tiles. There are numerous types of grout, and selecting the proper grouting material will depend upon the tile and conditions of the installation. Check with your tile dealer for selection of the proper grouting material.

CUTTING AND INSTALLING TILE

Methods for cutting and installing tile are determined by the type of tile and the conditions of the installation. Planning is a key element to good tile installations. Laying out the tile to obtain the proper pattern and spacing tiles evenly will take some thought. Tile cutters can be rented at tool rental centers. Some tile dealers will loan you the tile cutters when you purchase tile from them. A rod saw can be used to cut most tiles. Tile nippers are used to make small cuts on tile. Wet saws are the preferred tool of professionals for cutting tile.

Installation methods vary, and you should check with your dealer and follow the manufacturer's recommendations for the installation of your tile. I will give you an example of one way to install tile, but be advised, you may need to follow other procedures for the tile you choose.

Once you have planned your layout, trowel adhesive on the subfloor. Generally, the adhesive should have a thickness of about ¼ of an inch. You can purchase plastic spacers to help you maintain even spacing between your tiles. The spacers are in the shape of a cross and fit between the tiles. Lay your first tile in the center of the floor and lay subsequent tiles from that point.

As the tile is set in the adhesive, it should be pressed in firmly. Sometimes rubber hammers are used to tap the tile in. A regular hammer can be used if you lay a block of wood over the tile and tap on the wooden block. A long level is handy when checking the floor for consistency. Once the entire tile is set, you must wait for the next step. The length of time you have to wait is determined by the type of adhesive being used, so check the manufacturer's recommendations.

After the waiting period, you are ready to grout the tile. Check with your local tile dealer for the best type of grout to use with your tile. Follow manufacturer's recommendations. In general, the grout is mixed and spread over the floor, filling the gaps between the tiles. The grout is usually applied

TRADE TIP

Grout joints should be sealed. Not all installers seal their grout joints, but it is advisable to do so. This will help protect the grout and will reduce the risk of water running through the grout.

with a special trowel. Once the grout has filled the cracks, wash the remainder of the grout off with a wet sponge. It will probably be necessary to wet the grout over the following three days to allow it to set properly. Again, I want to remind you that there are many variables in tile work. Consult local professionals and follow manufacturer's suggestions.

HARDWOOD FLOORING

Hardwood flooring is expensive, but attractive. Once common, hardwood floors are now found only in upscale housing. This type of flooring is generally of a narrow, tongue-and-groove nature, and special tools make the installation easier. However, you might choose wide wood planks or small wood squares. There are many types and grades of hardwood flooring. Talk with your local supplier, and ask to see samples before making your buying decision. Let's move on and see how you might use hardwood floors in your project.

SUB-FLOORS

Sub-floors for hardwood flooring can take on many different characteristics. They can be made of plywood, boards, or sleeper joists. In most cases, the sub-floor will be plywood. The plywood should be at least ½ of an inch thick. It is important to have the sub-floor nailed tightly. It is a good idea to leave about ⅛ of an inch between the sheets of plywood. You can use nails driven into the joists as temporary spacers.

If you want to install hardwood floors over a concrete slab, you must consider the possibility of moisture problems. If water or extreme dampness seeps up through the concrete, the hardwood can warp and discolor. Even if you don't anticipate moisture problems, it is wise to install a vapor barrier on the slab. The vapor barrier can be a 4-mil plastic.

You can install the plastic vapor barrier on the slab and then lay sheets of exterior-grade plywood on the plastic, as a sub-floor. Powder-actuated nailing tools make quick work of nailing the ply-

TRADE TIP

Hardwood flooring can be difficult to install and finish. Special tools are needed when working with hardwood flooring. This is definitely one part of a project to give serious consideration to calling the professional help for.

wood to the concrete. If you opt for a sleeper system, install the sleepers on the concrete and drape the plastic over the strips of wood. If you are installing wood squares, similar to tile, you will still need to cover the sleepers with plywood. But, for planks and tongue-and-groove strips, you can eliminate the use of plywood.

FIGURE 14-3
Hardwood flooring is an expensive and attractive flooring choice, found mostly in upscale homes.

TONGUE-AND-GROOVE FLOORING

Tongue-and-groove flooring is usually sold in narrow strips, ranging from 1½ inches in width to just over three inches. The thickness of these strips is usually about ¾ of an inch. Length of strip flooring may range from nine inches to over eight feet.

> ### PRO POINTER
> If water or extreme dampness seeps up through concrete to a hardwood floor, the hardwood can warp and discolor. Even if you don't anticipate moisture problems, it is wise to install a vapor barrier on the slab. The vapor barrier can be a 4-mil plastic.

PLANK FLOORING

Plank flooring is generally not tongue-and-grooved, but it may be. This type of wood floor accentuates a country charm. It is normally about ¾ of an inch thick, with widths from three to eight inches.

FLOORING SQUARES

Flooring squares are a wood flooring material that resembles tile. The squares may be between 10 to 36 inches square. Rectangular shapes are also available. These hardwood tiles are generally installed with the use of an adhesive, in a fashion similar to tile installation.

THE FINISH

Hardwood flooring is commonly available with the finish already put on the wood. This may cost a little more, but for the average person, a pre-finished floor is a bargain. If you prefer to do your own sanding and finishing, unfinished flooring is also available.

NAILING

Nailing down hardwood flooring with a hammer and nails can get old, fast. Tool rental centers provide nailing devices that make the installation of the flooring much easier. The nailer will drive nails in at an angle, keeping them concealed from view. There is no need to pre-drill holes in the flooring when using a nailing device. If you elect to use a hammer and nails, pre-drill the nail holes.

The first strips of hardwood flooring are nailed from the top. Shoe molding will hide the nail holes. Pre-drill the holes and nail the first strip to the sub-floor. The grooved portion of the tongue-and-groove strip should be facing the wall. As the strips are installed, they are normally laid out in random lengths.

Nailing a plank flooring calls for different techniques. The planking will probably come with plugs to fill nail holes. If it doesn't, you will need a plug-cutter for your electric drill. Plank flooring is often installed with the use of recessed screws. Once the screws are in place, the wooden plugs are put in the holes to hide the screws.

FLOATING FLOORS

Floating floors have become very popular. These floors have an appearance that is close to that of a hardwood floor, but the flooring is easy to install. Prep work is similar to that required for vinyl flooring. Most types of floating floor have foam pads that go under the flooring. Then the floor basically snaps together in sections. Handy homeowners can install this flooring with professional results, and the flooring is very durable and easy to clean.

FINAL WORDS ON FLOORING

I have been in the construction and remodeling business for almost 30 years. I'm sure that with enough thought and effort I could install a floor to my liking, but I prefer to subcontract this phase of my jobs to professionals. There are many considerations and possible pitfalls to doing your own flooring. Weigh the advantages against the potential disadvantages carefully. If you feel good about doing the job, go for it. If you think you may be getting in over your head, don't feel embarrassed to call in a pro.

15

Setting Fixtures

Setting fixtures is one of the last aspects of your job. Just because you are nearing the end of your project, you cannot let your guard down. It is not uncommon for fixtures to be broken, floors to be damaged, or injuries to occur in this phase of the work. Most of the fixture work will involve light fixtures and plumbing fixtures, but heating units may also play a part in the setting of fixtures. Since we are so close to having the job finished, let's jump right into it.

PLUMBING FIXTURES

Plumbing fixtures are generally easy to install, but they can offer up some problems. We will look at each common household fixture and the proper method of installation. You will also be given some tips for staying out of trouble.

TRADE TIP
The top of a closet flange for a toilet installation should never be below the finished floor.

TOILETS

Professionals can assemble and set a new toilet in less than 15 minutes. If the rough-in is right, the job is easy. The first step is installing the closet flange, if it wasn't already installed during the rough-in. Closet flanges should generally sit on the sub-floor. If you are using a thick tile floor, the flange may need to be shimmed to raise it above the sub-floor. The top of the flange should never be below the finished floor.

With plastic pipe, the flange is glued into place. When setting the flange, be sure the grooves that will hold the closet bolts are in proper alignment. With most toilets the closet bolts should be set so that they are about 12 inches from the back wall. After the flange is installed, place the closet bolt under the grooved lips of the flange. Next, place a wax ring over the opening in the flange. The wax should be installed at room temperature. If the wax is too cold, it will not seal well. If necessary, warm the wax under a light, by a heater, or carefully with a torch, before installing it.

Once the closet bolts and wax ring are in place, set the bowl of the toilet onto the flange. The closet bolts should penetrate the holes in the base of the toilet. Push down on the toilet bowl. It may be necessary to straddle and sit on the bowl, facing the back wall, to have it set and compress the wax properly.

Measure from the back wall to the holes in the toilet where the seat will be installed. The two holes should be an equal distance from the back wall. If they are not, twist the toilet bowl until the holes are the same distance from the back wall.

Install the flat plastic caps that came with the toilet, over the closet bolts. If metal washers were packed with the closet bolts, install them next. Then, screw the nuts that came with the closet bolts onto the bolts. Use an adjustable wrench to tighten these nuts. Be careful when tightening the nuts, toilet bases are fragile and will break if too much stress is applied to them. You will know these bolts are tight enough when the toilet will not shift from side to side. Snap the plastic cover caps that came with the toilet over the bolts and onto the flat plastic disks you installed over the bolts. If the bolts are too long to allow the caps to seat, cut the bolts off with a hacksaw.

Uncrate the toilet tank and lay it on its back. Place the large sponge washer over the threaded piece that extends from the bottom of the tank, this piece is the base of the flush valve. Next, you will install the tank-to-bowl-bolts. Most toilets are set up to accept two tank-to-bowl bolts, but some are designed to accept three.

Slide the heavy black washers up over the bolts until they reach the head of the bolt. Push the bolts through the toilet tank. Now, pick the tank up and set it in place on the bowl. The sponge gasket

FIGURE 15-1
Toilet installation is a job most any handy homeowner can handle.

and bolts should line up with the holes in the bowl. If you have a helper, ask the helper to hold the tank while you tighten the bolts. If you don't have a helper, be careful not to allow the tank to fall. If the tank takes a tumble, it is likely to break.

Once the tank is in place, slide the metal washers over the tank-to-bowl bolts from beneath the bowl. Follow the washers with nuts and tighten them. Again, be careful, too much stress will crack the tank. Alternate between bolts as you tighten them. This allows the pressure to be applied evenly, reducing the change of an accidental breakage. Tighten these bolts until the tank is mounted on the bowl firmly.

Your next task is connecting the water to the toilet. This example is based on the use of copper tubing for water distribution piping. If you used CPVC or some other type of pipe, use normal installation methods to install the cut-off valve. Cut-off valves for fixtures are normally called stops.

First, make sure the water to the supply pipe is turned off. Then, cut the supply pipe off about ¾ of an inch above the floor or past the wall. Slide an escutcheon over the pipe. You can use stops that are held in place with soldered joints, but compression stops are easier and faster. Loosen the big nut on the compression stop and slide the stop onto the pipe. Use two adjustable wrenches to tighten the large nut. One wrench should be on the stop and the other should be on the large nut.

The next item you will need is a closet supply. You can use a chrome supply but PEX supplies are much easier to work with. Flexible supply tubes are also available for use by inexperienced plumbers and homeowners. In either case, remove the ballcock nut from the water supply connection at the bottom of the toilet tank. Place the head of the closet supply on the ballcock supply and bend the supply to a point where it would fit in the supply opening of the stop. Mark the supply tube and cut it. You can cut it with roller-cutters or a hacksaw.

DID YOU KNOW?

Toilets are fairly easy to assemble and install. Most any handy homeowner can do this job.

Slide the ballcock nut onto the supply tube, with the threads facing the toilet tank. Slide the small nut from the stop onto the supply tube and follow it with the compression ferrule. If you are using a PEX supply, use a nylon ferrule. Hold the supply up to the ballcock and run the ballcock nut up handtight. Insert the other end of the supply into the stop. Slide the ferrule down to the stop and tighten the small compression nut. Then, tighten the large ballcock nut.

Take the toilet seat from its box and install it. The seat will have built-in bolts that fit through holes in the bowl. Put the seat in place and tighten the nuts that hold it in place.

Turn the handle of the stop clockwise until it stops, this closes the valve. Turn the main water supply on. Open the stop valve by turning it counterclockwise. The toilet tank should fill with water. Once the tank is full, flush the toilet. Check around the base of the toilet for water. If water is present, you may have to pull and reset the toilet. Water around the base indicates a bad seal with the wax ring.

Check around the tank-to-bowl bolts for water. If you find any, gently tighten the nuts on these bolts and the water should stop dripping. Check the compression connections on the water supply. If they leak, tighten the nuts and the leak should cease.

LAVATORY TOPS

Lavatory tops are tops with the lavatory bowl built into the top. These tops sit on a vanity cabinet. Normally the tops are heavy enough to simply sit in place on the vanity. With small tops, it may be necessary to set them in a bed of adhesive on the cabinet.

Once the top is set, you are ready to hook up the lavatory. Many plumbers mount the lavatory faucets on the bowl before setting the top. This procedure is faster and easier than trying to do the job while scrunched up under the cabinet.

Some faucets come with a gasket that fits between the base of the faucet and the lavatory. If your faucet doesn't have such a gasket, make a gasket from plumber's putty. Roll the putty into a long round line and place it around the perimeter of the faucet base. Set the faucet on the top, with the threaded fittings going through the holes.

Remove the supply nuts from the ends of the threaded fittings. Slide the ridged washers over the threaded fittings of the faucet. Then, screw on the mounting nuts. Tighten these nuts until the faucet will not twist about on the top. Take two sink supply tubes and mount them to the bottom of the threaded fittings. This is done by sliding the supply nuts up the supply tubes and screwing them onto the threaded fittings. The beveled fit will prevent leaks. If you are working from inside the vanity, you will need a basin wrench to tighten the mounting and supply nuts.

Set the top into place, if you haven't already. Make sure the main water supply is turned off and install the cut-offs for the lavatory. Connect the supply tubes to the stops in the same fashion used on the toilet.

FIGURE 15-2
Bathroom sinks and faucets come in a wide variety of styles.

Now you are ready to connect the drainage. The first step is the assembly and installation of the pop-up drain assembly. There will be detailed instructions for the proper installation of these devices packed with the faucets. However, I will give you a general idea of what you are getting into.

TRADE TIP

Many plumbers mount the lavatory faucets on the bowl before setting the top. This procedure is faster and easier than trying to do the job while scrunched up under the cabinet.

The pop-up assembly is what goes in the hole in the bottom of the sink. When you look at your pop-up assembly it may appear confusing. Actually, the pop-up is easy to install.

Unscrew the round trim piece, the piece you are accustomed to seeing when you look into a lavatory, from the threaded body of the pop-up assembly. Roll up some plumber's putty and place a ring of it around the bottom of the trim piece. Slide the fat, tapered, black washer that is on the threaded portion of the assembly, down on the threaded shaft. You may have to loosen the big nut that is on the threads to get the metal washer and rubber washer to move down on the assembly.

Apply pipe dope, joint compound, or a sealant tape to the threads of the pop-up assembly. With your hand under the lavatory bowl, push the threaded assembly up through the drainage hole. Screw the small trim piece, the one with the putty on it, onto the threads. Push the tapered gasket up to the bottom of the lavatory. Tighten the mounting nut until it pushes the metal washer up to the rubber washer and compresses the rubber washer. You should notice putty being squeezed out from under the trim ring as you tighten the nut.

When the mounting nut is tight, the metal pop-up rod that extends from the assembly should be pointing to the rear of the lavatory bowl. Take the thin metal rod, the rod used to open and close the lavatory drain, and push it through the small hole in the center of the faucet.

You should see a thin metal clip on the end of the rod that extends from the pop-up assembly. Remove the first edge of this clip from the round rod. Take the perforated metal strip that was packed with the pop-up and slide it over the pop-up rod. You can use any of the holes for starters. Now, slide the edge of the thin metal clip back onto the pop-up rod, this will hold the perforated strip in place.

At the other end of the perforated strip there will be a hole and a setscrew. Loosen the setscrew and slide the pop-up rod, the rod used to open and close the drain, through the hole. Hold the rod so that about 1½ inches is protruding above the top of the faucet. Tighten the setscrew. Pull up on the pop-up rod and see that it operates the pop-up plug. The pop-up plug is the stopper in the sink drain. You can test this best after all connections are made to the water and drainage systems.

There should be a 1¼ inch chrome tailpiece, a round tubular piece, that was packed with the pop-up assembly. The tailpiece will have fine threads on one end and no threads on the other. Coat the threads with pipe dope or sealant tape. Screw the tailpiece into the bottom of the pop-up assembly.

Now you are ready to install the trap. First, slide an escutcheon over the trap arm, the piece of pipe stubbed out for the trap. Lavatory traps are normally 1¼ inch , however, you can use a 1½ inch trap with a reducing nut on the end that connects to the tailpiece. Assuming you used plastic pipe for your rough-in, you may either glue your trap directly to the trap arm, if you are using a schedule 40 trap, or you may use a trap adapter, if you are using a metal trap. Trap adapters glue onto pipe, just like any other fitting. One end of the adapter is equipped with threads, to accept a slip-nut.

Start by placing the trap on the tailpiece. To do this, remove the slip-nut from the vertical section of the trap. Slide the slip nut onto the tailpiece and follow it with the washer that was under it. The washer may be nylon or rubber. Put the trap on the tailpiece and check the alignment with the trap arm. It may be necessary to use a fitting to offset the trap arm in the direction of the trap.

PRO POINTER

Before testing a new faucet installation, you should remove the aerator from the faucet. This is the piece that screws into or onto the faucet spout. If you don't remove the aerator, it will often become blocked with debris and cause an erratic water stream. Once the aerator is removed, turn on the faucet and let it run for several minutes. Then turn the faucet off and replace the aerator.

If the trap is below the trap arm, you will have to shorten the tail-piece. The tailpiece is best cut with a pair of roller-cutters, but it can be cut with a hacksaw. You may have to remove the tailpiece to cut it. If the trap is too high, you can use a tailpiece extension to lower it. A tailpiece extension is a tubular section that fits between the trap and the tailpiece. The extension may be plastic or metal, and it is held in place with slip-nuts and washers.

Once the trap is at the proper height, you must determine if the trap arm needs to be cut or extended. Extending the trap arm can be done with a regular coupling and pipe section. If you are using a schedule 40 plastic trap, it is glued onto the trap arm. If you are using a metal trap, the long section of the trap will slip into a trap adapter. You may have to shorten the length of the trap's horizontal section. When using a trap adapter, slide the slip-nut and washer on the trap section. Then, insert the trap section into the adapter and secure it by tightening the slip-nut. Once the trap-to-trap-arm connection is complete, tighten the slip-nut at the tailpiece.

Your next job is to install the cut-offs. Use the same procedures described in the toilet section to accomplish this. Make sure the main water supply is turned off. Cut the pipe stubs and install escutcheons. Install the stops and connect the supply tubes to the stops. Make sure the stops are in the off position and turn the main water supply back on.

Remove the aerator from the faucet. This is the piece that screws into or onto the faucet spout. If you don't remove the aerator, it will often become blocked with debris and cause an erratic water stream. Make sure the faucet is turned off and open the stops. Close the drain of the lavatory by pulling up on the pop-up rod. Turn the left side of the faucet on and make sure it produces hot water. Hot should always be on the left and cold should be on the right. If for some reason you roughed your pipes in on the wrong sides, you can correct the problem by using long supply tubes and crossing them under the lavatory.

Fill the lavatory with water. If the bowl will not hold the water, adjust the pop-up controls. Getting the pop-up set in the right holes and at the proper height may take a little trial-and-error experimentation, but you can do it. Release the water in the bowl and check all drainage fittings for leaks. If there are leaks at slip-nuts, tightening the nuts should solve the problem. If you have a leak at a threaded connection, try tightening the threads, but you may have to remove the piece and install additional pipe dope or tape.

DROP-IN LAVATORIES

Drop-in lavatories differ only in the way the bowl is installed. The waste and water connections for all lavatories are essentially the same. Drop-in lavatories are so named because they simply drop into a countertop. A hole is cut in the top that is slightly smaller than the rim diameter of the lavatory. Caulking is applied around the edge of the hole, on the top of the counter. The drop-in lavatory is set into place and connected to the drain and water supply. There are no special mounting brackets or clips; the weight of the lavatory holds it in place.

RIMMED LAVATORIES

Rimmed lavatories are not very popular. These are the lavatories that have a metal ring surrounding them, the ring that collects dirt and is hard to clean around. Installing a rimmed lavatory requires cutting a hole in the countertop, using a template supplied with the lavatory. The metal ring is set in the hole. Then, the lavatory is installed from below the countertop. The bowl is held up from below, until it comes into contact with the ring. Special clips are used to hold the bowl in place. The clips fit in a channel that runs around the metal ring. As the clips are tightened, they apply pressure on the bottom of the lavatory rim. These lavatories can be a pain to install, especially without help.

WALL-HUNG LAVATORIES

Wall-hung lavatories hang on a wall bracket. When wall-hung lavatories will be used, wood backing must be installed during the rough-in phase. The backing, a two-by-eight, is nailed between two studs. The backing provides a solid place to install screws that will support the wall bracket.

In the trim-out phase, the wall bracket is hung and secured with screws or lag bolts. The directions that come with wall-hung lavatories should give the proper height for the bracket. The top of the bracket will normally be about 30 or 31 inches off the floor. As you secure the bracket, make sure it remains level.

TRADE TIP
When wall-hung lavatories will be used, wood backing must be installed during the rough-in phase. The backing, a two-by-eight, is nailed between two studs. The backing provides a solid place to install screws that will support the wall bracket.

Once the bracket is installed, the lavatory is placed on the bracket. Be sure the lavatory is seated firmly on the bracket before turning it loose. If the bowl falls, it is likely to break. Once on the bracket, check the bowl for level. You may have to use the heel of your hand to tap the lavatory down on one end or the other, until it is level.

Some wall-hung units have holes in them for additional lag bolts. These holes allow lag bolts to be run through the lavatory after it is on the bracket, ensuring that it will not be knocked off the bracket. However, not all wall-hung bowls have these extra holes.

TUB AND SHOWER TRIM

The tub and shower trim for a faucet is easy to install. However, installing a tub waste is difficult, unless you have help. Let's take a look at what is required for trimming out your tub or shower.

SHOWER TRIM

Shower trim is easy to install. Start with the shower head. Be sure the main water supply is turned off and unscrew the stub-out from the shower-head ell. Slide the escutcheon that came with the shower assembly over the shower arm. Apply pipe dope or tape to the threads on each end of the shower arm. Screw the shower head on the short section of the arm, where the bend is. Screw the long section of the arm into the threaded ell in the wall.

Use an adjustable wrench on the flats around the shower head to tighten all connections. If you must use pliers on the arm, keep them close to the wall so that the escutcheon will hide scratch marks.

Now you are ready to trim out the shower valve. How this is done will depend on the type of faucet you roughed-in. Follow manufacturer's suggestions. If you installed a single-handle unit, you will normally install the large escutcheon first. These escutcheons normally incorporate the use of a foam gasket, removing the need for plumber's putty. Then the handle is installed and the cover cap is snapped into place over the handle screw. If you are using a two-handle faucet, you will normally screw in chrome collars over the faucet stems. These may be followed by escutcheons or the escutcheons may be an integral part of the sleeves. Putty should be placed where the escutcheons come into contact with the tub wall. Then the handles are installed.

TUB FAUCETS

Tub faucets are trimmed out in the same way as shower faucets. However, you will have a tub spout to install. Some tub spouts slide over a piece of copper tubing and are held in place with a set screw. Many tub spouts have a female-threaded connection, either at the inlet or the outlet of the spout. If you are dealing with a threaded connection, you must solder a male adapter onto the stub-out from your tub valve or use a threaded ell and galvanized nipple. The type of spout that slides over the copper and attaches with a set screw are by far the easiest to install. You should place plumber's putty on the tub spout, where it comes into contact with the tub wall.

TUB WASTES

Tub wastes are difficult to install when you are working alone. The tub waste and overflow can take several forms. It may be made of metal or plastic. It can use a trip lever, a push button, a twist-and-turn stopper, or an old-fashioned rubber stopper. The tub waste may go together with slip-nuts or glued joints. Follow the directions that come with your tub waste.

The first step for installing a tub waste is the mounting of the drain. Unscrew the chrome drain from the tub shoe. You will see a thick black washer. Install a ring of putty around the chrome drain, and apply pipe dope to the threads. Hold, or better yet, have your assistant hold, the tub shoe under the tub, so that it lines up with the drain hole. Screw the chrome drain into the female threads of the shoe. The black washer should be on the bottom of the tub, between the tub and the shoe. Once the chrome drain is handtight, leave it alone, for now.

The tub shoe has a tubular drainage pipe extending from it. Make this drain point towards the head of the tub, where the faucets are installed. Take the tee that came with the tub waste and put it on the drainage tube from the shoe. Then, take the long drainage tube that will accept the tub's overflow, and place it in the top of the tee. You want the face of the overflow tube to line up with the overflow hole in the tub. Cut the tubing on the overflow or shoe tubing as needed. The cuts are best made with roller-cutters, but can be made with a hack saw.

You should have a sponge gasket in your assortment of parts. This gasket will be placed on the face of the overflow tubing, between the back of the tub and the overflow head. From inside the bathtub, install the face plate for the overflow. For trip-lever styles, you will have to fish the trip mechanism down the overflow tubing. For other types of tub wastes, you will only have a cover plate to screw on. Tighten the screws until the sponge gasket is compressed.

> **TRADE TIP**
> Tub wastes are difficult to install when you are working alone. Homeowners can do this type of work, but the job is much easier when there are two people involved in completing the task.

Now, tighten the drain. This can be done by crossing two large screwdrivers and using them between the crossbars of the drain. Turn the drain clockwise until the putty spreads out from under the drain.

The last step is connecting the tub waste to the trap. This can be done with trap adapters or glue joints, depending upon the type of tub waste you have used.

Apply joint compound to the threads of the tailpiece, if you're using a metal waste, and screw the tailpiece into place. From this point on, it is just like hooking up a lavatory drain.

KITCHEN SINKS

Kitchen sinks are similar to lavatories, but they have their differences. Here, we are going to explore those differences.

MOUNTING THE SINK

Mounting the kitchen sink is normally done in one of two ways. Some kitchen sinks are drop-ins. Like lavatories, drop-in sinks don't require clips, only caulking. Most sinks, however, are held in place with clips. These clips slide into a channel that runs around the rim of the sink. As the clips are tightened, usually with a screwdriver, the clips bite into the bottom of the countertop, pulling the sink firmly into contact with the top of the counter. There are different types of sink clamps, so check your materials and manufacturer's instructions for proper installation.

BASKET STRAINERS

Instead of pop-up assemblies, kitchen sinks utilize basket strainers for drains. Putty is applied around the rim of the drain and the drain is pushed through the hole in the sink. From below, a fiber gasket is slid over the threaded portion of the drain and a large nut is applied and tightened. These nuts can be difficult to tighten without help. It is best to have someone cross screwdrivers in the crossbars of the basket strainer as the nut is being tightened. Otherwise, the entire drain assembly tends to turn, without becoming tight.

A good solution for the person working alone is a type of drain that uses a flange to secure the basket strainer. With this type of arrangement, the flange slides over the threads and is held against the bottom of the sink by three pressure points. The pressure points are threaded rods extending from another flange that is screwed onto the drain threads. As the threaded rods are tightened, they apply pressure and seal the drain.

TAILPIECES

Kitchen tailpieces do not screw into the basket strainers. Instead, they are flanged to accept tailpiece washers. The nylon washer sits on top of the tailpiece and the tailpiece is held in place with a slip-nut.

CONTINUOUS WASTES

Since many kitchen sinks have two bowls, continuous wastes are often used to drain the two bowls to a common trap. There are end-outlet wastes and center-outlet wastes. The continuous waste attaches to the sink's tailpieces with slip-nuts and washers. Then, the waste tubes run either to a tee, for an end-outlet waste or a double tee, for a center outlet waste. The bottoms of these tees accept a tailpiece and allow the trap to be attached.

FIGURE 15-3
A wet bar in the kitchen area is a popular choice.

GARBAGE DISPOSERS

When garbage disposers are used, they are mounted to the kitchen sink. A garbage disposer takes the place of a basket strainer. Putty is applied to the ring of the disposer's trim piece. The trim is pushed through the drain hole. A pressure-type flange is put over the collar of the drain and followed by a snap ring. The snap ring holds the pressure flange in place. Threaded rods are tightened with a screwdriver, to seal the drain. Then, the disposer is held into place. A rotating collar is turned to lock onto the disposer.

The disposer has a small ell that comes with it. Two screws are loosened on the side of the disposer. The ell fits through a metal housing and a rubber washer is placed on the beveled end of the ell, the short end. The metal housing it put back in place and the screws are tightened. This compresses the gasket between the face of the ell and the side of the disposer. Then, the continuous waste or trap is connected to the bottom of the disposer ell.

DISHWASHERS

Dishwashers are normally installed under the countertop, between cabinets. There are metal tabs at the top of the dishwasher that allow screws to be installed to hold the appliance in place. A rubber drain hose connects to a ridged nylon drain on the appliance. The hose is held in place by a snap ring or clamp. This hose should run into the sink base and rise to the top of the enclosure. It should connect to an air gap with clamps.

An air gap is a device that sits on the counter and has a chrome cover. It is installed by removing the chrome cover and mounting nut. The unit is pushed up through its hole from beneath the counter. Then the gasket and mounting nut are installed and tightened. Afterwards, the chrome cover is replaced. Below the counter, the air gap splits off into a wye.

The small hose from the dishwasher connects to one side of the wye and is held in place with a clamp. Then, a larger hose is run from the other section of the wye to a wye-tailpiece connection or a connection point on a disposer. If you are connecting to a disposer, you must knock out the factory-installed plug before connecting the hose. This can be done with a sturdy screwdriver and a hammer. You should knock this plug out before installing the disposer; otherwise, retrieving the knocked-out plug will be difficult.

DID YOU KNOW?

Did you know that all dishwashers should be installed with an air gap in the drainage system? Well, they should. This is a safety device that should not be excluded from any dishwasher installation.

To connect the water supply to the dishwasher, you will need to used a dishwasher stop or cut a tee into the hot-water supply to the sink. A dishwasher stop has provisions for a supply tube to the sink and the tubing running to the dishwasher. The copper tubing for the dishwasher should be equipped with a cut-off valve. If you use a dishwasher stop, you have a built-in cut-off. If you cut in a tee, install a stop-and-waste valve between the tee and the dishwasher tubing.

The tubing will run to a point under the dishwasher. A dishwasher ell is used to make the connection between the tubing and the dishwasher. The dishwasher ell screws into the dishwasher. Use pipe dope or tape on the threads. The tubing connects to the ell with a compression nut and ferrule.

BAR SINKS

You can think of bar sinks as miniature kitchen sinks. The installation procedures are essentially the same.

FAUCETS

When selecting faucets that you plan to install yourself, choose faucets that are all in one piece. Some designer-type faucets come with the handles and spout as individual units. For the homeowner, putting these delicate and sometimes intricate faucets together can be troublesome.

HEATING TRIM

Heating trim is relatively easy to install. In the case of a forced-air system, all you have to do is set registers into the duct work. You will cut out the section of flooring that is covering the duct opening and insert the registers. Keep your flooring cuts smaller than the register. A mistake in sizing your hole can cause considerable trouble.

With hot-water baseboard units, the work is more complex, but still manageable. Hot-water heat generally consists of copper tubing with fins on it. You will have stubs roughed-in. Turn the water to the stubs off and begin your installation. The installation is a matter of screwing the baseboard units to the wall and soldering the copper connection. Splicers are available for joining baseboard units in long runs. These splicers are merely a trim piece that hides the seam where two pieces of heat butt together. End caps will be installed at each end of the heat to hide valves, ells, and the exposed ends of heating elements.

If you are installing hot-water baseboard that is on its own zone, you will need to mount a thermostat. Thermostats are normally mounted chest-high, and they must be level to function properly. Some thermostats are set up for a two-wire system and others for a three-wire system. Buy a thermostat that will match your wiring. The thermostat may be for a 24-volt system or it could be for a 750-millivolt system. Confirm your needs and make sure the thermostat you purchase will work with your existing conditions.

When mounting the thermostat, remove the cover. The back of the unit is the mounting surface. You will see holes in the back casing of the unit. Screw the base to the wall, making sure that it remains level. Connect wiring in accordance with the wiring diagram supplied with your equipment. Replace the cover, and you should be all set.

Electric baseboard heat will be connected electrically and screwed to the wall. Remember to have the power turned off when working with the wiring.

ELECTRICAL FIXTURES AND DEVICES

Electrical fixtures are not difficult to install, but caution must be observed. Always be sure the wires you are working with are not hot with electricity. Fixtures are generally lights. Devices are normally outlets and switches.

WIRING DEVICES

When installing wiring devices, be absolutely sure the power to the circuits you are working with is off. You will use a knife and a wire stripper to prepare the ends of your roughed-in wiring for the connection to devices. There is a color-code system that should be followed when installing your electrical devices. Green wires or bare copper wires should be used as a ground wire. Red wires should be considered hot wires and normally attach to brass or chrome screws. Black wires are also considered hot and generally attach to brass screws. In many cases white wires serve as a neutral wire and connect to chrome screws, but don't count on white wires not being hot.

> **PRO POINTER**
>
> Unless you are experienced in working with electrical wiring, I strongly suggest that you contract a licensed electrician to perform all of your wiring needs.

There are times when the white wires are used as a black wire. Most electricians will wrap black tape around the white wire to indicate its use a hot wire. However, you can never assume anything when working with electricity. If you have reason to use a white wire as a black wire, wrap it with black tape or tag it in some way to indicate its use.

Some receptacles are made to allow wires to be stuck into them, rather than being placed under screws. Most professionals frown on this practice and prefer to secure wires under screws. When you crook the end of wires to fit under screws, bend the wires so the crook will tighten as the screw is tightened. For example, as you are holding the wire, bend the crook so the end of the wire curls to your right.

When joining two wires to each other, use wire nuts. Wire nuts come in various sizes, to fit different size wires. The nuts have a plastic exterior and a metal spring on the inside. It is a good idea to twist wires together before installing the wire nuts. Place the wire nut over the wires and turn the nut clockwise. As you turn the nut, the connection between the wires is secured with the spring and the nut becomes attached tightly to the wires. Make sure all bare wiring is concealed in the wire nut.

Most metal electrical boxes will have a green screw for the ground wire to be mounted under. Some electricians use a ground clip. Ground clips are just thin metal clips that slide over the edge of a metal box and bring the ground wire into contact with the metal.

If your wiring includes a bathroom, plan on installing a ground-fault receptacle or circuit breaker. Check local code requirements for the required location of the ground-fault interceptor (GFI) outlet.

WALL PLATES AND SWITCH COVERS

Wall plates and switch covers simply mount over outlet boxes and switch boxes. They are held in place with screws.

LIGHT FIXTURES

Light fixtures are not particularly difficult to install. It is usually a matter of matching up the feed wires with the fixture wires and mounting the fixture. Most fixtures will have threaded studs that hold them to their electrical box. Consult the directions that come with your light fixtures and follow the manufacturer's recommendations.

WORKING IN THE PANEL BOX

I believe working in the panel box is too dangerous for the average person to attempt. With the fatal possibilities of working with electricity, I feel inexperienced people should rely on licensed professionals to inspect all work and complete the connections at the panel box.

IN CLOSING

In closing, I want to remind you to know your limitations. Not all people can do all jobs. There is no shame in calling in a professional. Study what your job requirements are and how well you are qualified to perform the work. When in doubt, call a professional.

Index

Page numbers in italics refer to figures